Evaluating School Programs

Third Edition

Evaluating School Programs

An Educator's Guide

Third Edition

James R. Sanders • Carolyn D. Sullins

CORWIN PRESS
A SAGE Publications Company
Thousand Oaks, California

For information:

Corwin Press
A Sage Publications Company
2455 Teller Road
Thousand Oaks, California 91320
www.corwinpress.com

Sage Publications Ltd.
1 Oliver's Yard
55 City Road
London EC1Y 1SP
United Kingdom

Sage Publications India Pvt. Ltd.
B-42, Panchsheel Enclave
Post Box 4109
New Delhi 110 017 India

Printed in the United States of America

Library of Congress Cataloging-in-Publication Data

Sanders, James R.
Evaluating school programs: An educator's guide / James R. Sanders,
Carolyn D. Sullins.—3rd ed.
        p. cm.
Includes bibliographical references and index.
ISBN 978-1-4129-2523-5 (cloth) — ISBN 978-1-4129-2524-2 (pbk.)
    1. Educational evaluation—United States—Handbooks, manuals, etc. I. Sullins,
Carolyn D. II. Title.
LB2822.75.S26 2006
379.1'58—dc22   2005015861

This book is printed on acid-free paper.

08   09   10   9   8   7   6   5   4   3   2

Acquisitions Editor:	Elizabeth Brenkus
Editorial Assistants:	Candice L. Ling and Desirée Enayati
Production Editor:	Laureen Shea
Copy Editor:	Barbara Coster
Typesetter:	C&M Digitals (P) Ltd.
Proofreader:	Kristin Bergstad
Indexer:	Kay Dusheck
Cover Designer:	Lisa Miller

Contents

Acknowledgments

We want to acknowledge the role that the late Dr. Richard Jaeger played in the creation of this book. The first edition was written at his request as part of his project funded by the Georgia Department of Education. Dick was very supportive and a wonderful critic and editor as the first edition took shape.

We appreciate the staff of the Evaluation Center at Western Michigan University for their assistance and support with all three editions. We especially thank Christine Hummel, Quentin Witkowski, and Christine Ellis for their invaluable help with this third edition.

We'd also like to thank Corwin Press, as well as the many educators we have worked with, for continuing to support developmental efforts such as this one. We need such means to share our experiences with other educators.

Finally, we want to thank our families—Susan, Jamie, and Jen, and Chris, Emily, and Kira—for their willingness to allow us to take time away from them to complete this third edition.

—James R. Sanders
—Carolyn D. Sullins
Kalamazoo, Michigan

Corwin Press gratefully acknowledges the contributions of the following reviewers:

Shelby Cosner, Senior Teaching Assistant, Doctoral Candidate
Department of Educational Leadership & Policy Analysis
University of Wisconsin-Madison, Madison, WI

Lizanne DeStefano, Associate Dean for Research
Bureau of Educational Research
University of Illinois at Urbana-Champaign, Champaign, IL

Mary Johnstone, 2004 NAESP National Distinguished Principal
Susitna Elementary School, Anchorage, AK

Beverly Parsons, Executive Director, Author
Insites, Dillon, CO

Jerry Vaughn, 2004 NAESP National Distinguished Principal
Central Elementary School, Cabot, AR

About the Authors

**James R. Sanders** is Professor Emeritus of Education and former Associate Director of the Evaluation Center at Western Michigan University. He received his master's degree in educational research from Bucknell University and his PhD in educational research and evaluation from the University of Colorado. He has served as a visiting professor at St. Patrick's College (in Dublin, Ireland), Utah State University, and the University of British Columbia. He is coauthor of *Educational Evaluation: Theory and Practice* (1973), *Practices and Problems in Competency-Based Measurement* (1979), *Educational Evaluation: Alternative Approaches and Practical Guidelines* (1987), and *Program Evaluation* (1997, 3rd ed., 2004). He is author or coauthor of numerous articles, monographs, and technical reports in the area of program evaluation. His articles have appeared in *Review of Educational Research, Educational Researcher, Educational and Psychological Measurement, Journal of Educational Psychology, Journal of School Psychology, New Directions for Program Evaluation, Evaluation News, Educational Technology, Journal of Research and Development in Education, Educational Measurement,* and *American Journal of Evaluation.*

Dr. Sanders has served as director or codirector of training institutes in evaluation for the American Educational Research Association, the American Evaluation Association, the Association for Supervision and Curriculum Development, and the Western Michigan University Evaluation Center. He has served as a member of the board of directors for the Evaluation Network and the American Evaluation Association and on standing committees for the American Educational Research Association, the National Council on Measurement in Education, the National Science Foundation, Phi Delta Kappa, Independent Sector, and the United Way of America. He has directed research and evaluation projects funded by the U.S. Department of Defense, U.S. Department of Education, National Science Foundation, and several state agencies. He has consulted with numerous school districts, private industries, instructional businesses, government agencies, research and development corporations, community agencies, and major universities. From 1988 to 1998, he served as Chair of the Joint Committee on Standards for Educational Evaluation, a coalition of 16 professional organizations concerned with the quality of evaluations done in education. He was elected by the American Evaluation Association to serve as President in 2001. In 2000, he received the Distinguished Services Award from Western Michigan University and the Friend of Evaluation Award from the Michigan Association for Evaluation.

 **Carolyn D. Sullins** is Senior Research Associate at the Evaluation Center at Western Michigan University. She has directed the evaluations of an afterschool program, a school-based behavior management program, and a parent information resource center. She was the project manager for the Cleveland Community Schools evaluation and has contributed to evaluations of charter schools in Illinois, Pennsylvania, and Michigan. In addition, she was the project director for the evaluation of a university alcohol risk-reduction project. Recently she has taught several graduate-level courses in program evaluation, including coteaching with Dr. Daniel Stufflebeam an advanced seminar in evaluation models.

Dr. Sullins earned her PhD in educational psychology in 2000, specializing in quantitative and evaluative research methods, at the University of Illinois at Urbana-Champaign, where she also completed her master's degree in counseling psychology in 1996. Her master's thesis, portions of which are published in *Psychology of Women Quarterly,* involved designing, administering, and analyzing a survey of therapists' practices. Her doctoral dissertation concerned an empowerment evaluation of a consumer-run mental health drop-in center. It involved mental health consumers in the design, implementation, interpretation, and use of an evaluation of their own center. This project, which generated five national presentations and an article in *American Journal of Evaluation,* led to new conceptualizations of particular evaluation models and applications.

Introduction

The Purpose of This Guide and How to Use It

This guide is intended for use by teachers and administrators in elementary and secondary school systems to help them evaluate their school programs. Evaluation is a complex process, and there is always the danger of oversimplification in a guide such as this. Please remember, evaluation is not a mechanical process; it is a human endeavor, and it carries with it all of the complexities and challenges of any human undertaking, including education.

There are two things above all else that one should remember about evaluating school programs. First, not everyone will see the program in the same light, and it is important to be informed about how those around you view it—its purpose, its approaches, who is involved and excluded, its costs and trade-offs, its accomplishments, its short-term and long-term future, and other things of interest to those who care about and are affected by the program. Second, one must always consider three aspects of good program evaluation—communication, communication, and communication. As long as you listen and respond, share information, discuss your intentions and obtain feedback, clarify expectations, provide clear and useful reports in a timely manner, and maintain an open evaluation process, the evaluation seas should be smooth.

This guide was written to provide basic program evaluation principles and procedures to aid educators in planning and conducting evaluations of school programs. Examples will help the reader to develop competence and confidence in program evaluation. Beyond this guide, however, indispensable experiences will be gained by undertaking evaluations and sharing your experiences with a nearby group of people with whom evaluation issues can be discussed. In addition, there are other evaluation resource materials that go into greater depth on many of the topics covered here. It is not possible to provide in this volume all of the detailed coverage of evaluation topics that some would like. For this reason, references to more advanced or specialized resources are provided (see Resource A and References).

This is a general guide that can be used to help plan any school program evaluation. The evaluation approach we have taken is one of many that could be used. This approach, however, is one that in our experience has worked well for school staff. Other approaches to school program evaluation that may be familiar to educators, such as accreditation and objectives-based evaluation, are described in reference works published by Fitzpatrick, Sanders, and Worthen (2004), Patton (1997), and Stufflebeam (2001).

The general principles in this guide are based on the advice of Daniel Stufflebeam (1969), who suggested that we must always attend to five tasks when conducting program evaluations:

1. Focusing the evaluation (see Chapter 2)

2. Collecting information (see Chapter 3)

3. Organizing and analyzing information (see Chapter 4)

4. Reporting information (see Chapter 5)

5. Administering the evaluation (see Chapter 6)

This guide will take you through the five tasks of school program evaluation, providing examples along the way. Use the guide as a reference book; it should not be read as a novel and then discarded. Program evaluation does not need to be complex or inordinately time consuming. It does not require extensive technical training. What it does require is *a desire* to improve one's school, *a willingness* to work collegially, careful *attention to detail,* and *basic knowledge* of how school program evaluations should be carried out. This guide provides the last of these key elements.

Why Evaluate Your School Programs?

This is a legitimate question. After all, aren't teachers and other school staff busy enough trying to educate students? Aren't there enough distractions already: dealing with parents, addressing disciplinary issues, attending endless professional development sessions, and so on, and so on? Besides, with federal mandates such as No Child Left Behind, there's already more than enough evaluation going on! There's no time left behind to even consider additional tasks!

DEFINITION OF EVALUATION

The reality is that successful program development—whether the program involves a new science curriculum, a parent-teacher organization, or a character development program—cannot occur without evaluation. Program evaluation is the process of systematically determining the quality of a program and how it can be improved.

The evaluation principles included in this guide provide a means for improvement and a way of documenting results so that others can learn from one's successes and failures. This way, precious time and resources can be delegated effectively. Indeed, any evaluation that is worth doing must ultimately *save* a school's time and resources and produce better results.

USES OF EVALUATION

Evaluation gives direction to everything that we do when changing and improving school programs. It is the process used to identify student needs. It is the process used to set priorities among needs and to translate needs into program objectives or modifications of existing objectives. It is the process used to identify and to select among different program approaches, organizations, staff assignments, materials and equipment, facilities, schedules, and other structuring choices in order to build a program that has a high likelihood of success. It is the process used to monitor and adjust programs as they are implemented. It is the process used to determine whether a program is resulting in desired outcomes and why the outcomes are as they are. It is the process used by outsiders to determine whether a program should be supported, changed, or terminated. It is the process used to judge requests for resources to support the program. In short, evaluation is an essential part of the improvement of school programs. It should underlie all changes and reforms. Without evaluation, change is blind and must be taken on faith.

BENEFITS OF EVALUATION

The payoffs of program evaluation are benefits to school staff and the children they serve. For example, as a result of sound program evaluation, benefits that can accrue to students might include improvement of educational practices and procedures or development of support materials to eliminate curricular weaknesses. Benefits to teachers might include recognition and support for teachers associated with a good program or help in choosing the best curriculum materials. Benefits to principals might include direction in setting priorities for school improvement or the identification and justification of needs for new programs.

FORMAL VERSUS INFORMAL EVALUATION

The process of evaluation involves two basic acts: (1) gathering information so that decisions will be informed and supportable and (2) applying criteria to the available information to arrive at justifiable decisions. The process is done systematically and openly so that others can follow along and all can learn. It is recorded in reports or other documents so that the steps in a decision process about a program can be traced, and, when necessary, the results can be reviewed and communicated clearly and accurately. Evaluation findings are reported in writing so that learning can be shared and made available for future use by others.

The evaluation process differs in important ways from the day-to-day personal decisions you make. When you evaluate items on a lunch menu, you do not systematically conduct an analytical study; you do not carefully collect data, analyze it, and report it; you do not explicitly describe the criteria that you are using to make a selection. You just do it. It is highly subjective and not open to public review and debate. One set of values applies. The results are not written up for future use or for sharing with others.

The evaluation of school programs frequently involves a much more rigorous process, because the decisions being made can affect many others—perhaps even the well-being of the next generation. Many perspectives need to be considered, and standards must be met. Formal reports are prepared and made public. This is what we mean by formal evaluation.

The Hammer of NCLB

When school staff think of evaluation, No Child Left Behind (NCLB) often pops into mind—often with an accompanying sense of anxiety and/or resentment. NCLB is neither the magic bullet hailed by its proponents nor the "Weapon of Mass Destruction" cursed by its detractors (Bracey, 2004). Arguably, NCLB isn't a weapon but a tool: a tool that, like a hammer, can be used to build or destroy.

However, we've all heard the expression "When all you have is a hammer, everything looks like a nail." Unfortunately, many educators feel they have been "nailed" by NCLB, without the benefit of other, perhaps more appropriate, forms of evaluation. With a greater variety of tools in one's evaluation toolbox, including those required by NCLB, a school can be assessed more accurately and eventually built stronger and more effective.[1]

ILLUSTRATIVE CASE STUDY (PART 1)

Before moving on, let's look at an illustrative case application of the material that we have covered. Although fictitious, this case is like many faced by building teachers and principals. Its purpose is to show how the evaluation steps could work in a real school setting. First, a scenario is presented, and then we will apply what has been discussed so far to the scenario. This illustrative case will be continued through the remainder of this guide. As each step in the program evaluation process is discussed, we will return to this case to examine how the discussion could be applied.

Setting of the Case Study

Lakeview City has a population of just over 50,000 people and is located midway between two major metropolitan areas, each about 200 miles away. Lakeview City is the county seat and the largest town within 100 miles. It has diversified industry, including a major chemical plant and the farm machinery division of a large national manufacturing company. The town is primarily blue-collar workers; however, unemployment has recently doubled, as the local chemical plant has dramatically downsized. There are about 8,000 students in Grades K–12. The school district has six elementary schools (Grades K–5), three middle schools (Grades 6–8), and two high schools (Grades 9–12). About 30% of the high school graduates go on to higher education, with the remainder taking jobs or going into the military. Approximately 10% of entering high school freshmen fail to finish high school.

The Purpose

In response to a new federal mandate, the state has recently begun statewide testing in science in Grades 4, 8, and 11. Last year Lakeview students at all three levels scored poorly on the science tests that were given; this meant that they failed to make Adequate Yearly Progress (AYP) as a district. While science test scores were below par in general, scores for low-income students were significantly lower than those for other students. Lakeview Elementary School had particularly poor scores on their fourth-grade science tests; while their test scores in reading and math had made some progress, the science scores had actually decreased. This puzzled the staff, because all of the school's curricula, including the science curriculum, had recently been updated to be in line with the new state standards. Furthermore, there seemed to be fewer complaints from or about the science department than other departments.

The principal, Ms. Goss, and the teachers were painfully aware of the consequences of not meeting AYP. At this point, it required developing a School Improvement Plan that targeted the school's weak areas. If the school continued to fail in meeting AYP, ultimately Ms. Goss could lose her job and the school could be restructured or even closed down and reopened as a charter school. Ms. Goss presented the results of the tests to a schoolwide team meeting of teachers, with predictable reactions.

Ms. Lee, a fourth-grade teacher protested, "Our low-income students, with all their socioeconomic limitations, can't possibly live up to such high standards!"

"Economics are no excuse," retorted Ms. Garcia, a third-grade teacher. "It's their parents, who just don't value education or discipline. If they can't parent, we can't teach!"

"It's just a few bad apples, really," explained another teacher. "Too bad we can't just make sure they're all absent the day of the tests."

Ms. Garcia chortled, "Hey, it's easy enough to rile them all up into a fist-fight with each other. Then we can expel them all. Problem solved!" Devious snickers ensued.

"The so-called bad apples alone couldn't have created overall science tests scores that were *this* low," Ms. Goss countered. "Besides, reading and math scores actually increased. We've got to focus on improving our science program, not blaming our kids."

"The sad part is," sighed Ms. Cooper, a fourth-grade teacher, "I was really looking forward to continuing that environmental science curriculum. Even the difficult kids seemed engaged with it. I hope we aren't forced to scrap it and teach to the test instead."

Ms. Lee rolled her eyes and hissed, "That NCLB is a bunch of B.S. Its one-size-fits-all approach is a totally inappropriate way to evaluate *our* unique school!"

Ms. Goss interrupted the gripe session. "I agree there are plenty of limitations to these tests, but they did point out that our science program isn't up to par. With all our attention on the reading program and the new discipline committee, we'd lost sight of that. That's what NCLB expects of us: to establish a School Improvement Plan to improve our weaknesses. And conducting our own internal evaluation—one that looks beyond narrow NCLB criteria—is the first step of that improvement plan. Otherwise, we're shooting in the dark."

What should be evaluated in schools? Chapter 2 presents an initial inventory of things that deserve evaluation. It also provides a process for identifying what to look at when evaluating a school program.

Internal Evaluation in Charter Schools: Key to Successful Schools and School Reform

Charter school advocates emphasize reduced bureaucracy, increased flexibility, opportunities to innovate, and accountability for student performance as essential to school reform (Chubb & Moe, 1990). Although charter schools are encouraged to demonstrate their achievements through unique methods as well as mandated traditional achievement tests, they rarely take advantage of the former. Various charter school studies have found that self-evaluation in charter schools is lacking, and that even their self-stated goals are often vague and immeasurable (Crew & Anderson, 2003; Legislative Office of Education Oversight, 2003; Sullins & Miron, 2005). Often schools simply lack the ability and resources to develop measurable goals and sound evaluation plans, but with assistance they can demonstrate their achievements through a variety of venues (Miron & Horn, 2002; Sullins & Miron, 2005).

Charter schools may be under even more pressure than traditional public schools to demonstrate good performance and family satisfaction, as they could lose their charter and cease to exist if they don't live up to the expectations set up in their charter. Although theoretically a charter school could lose its charter solely on the basis of not meeting its NCLB standards, this has been quite rare thus far. Charter school failures and closures have usually been the result of fiscal mismanagement, poor organization, and/or low enrollment: factors that can be proactively avoided by conducting continuous internal evaluation. Internal evaluation not only can prevent disastrous blunders, but it can assess progress on unique goals and objectives in addition to externally mandated ones. A school that fails to meet NCLB standards shows a greater chance of retaining its charter if it can demonstrate that it met its other unique goals and objectives. Fortunately, the smaller size, reduced bureaucracy, unifying mission, and familylike climate reduce the political gridlock that often occurs in larger school districts. These factors all facilitate internal evaluation.

Ideally, all schools—charter, traditional public, or private—must explore reasons for success or failure in meeting the goals and develop plans for continuing their successes and correcting their shortcomings. This is what helps schools become "learning organizations" that continually evaluate themselves and strive toward improvement (Awsumb-Nelson, 2001; Davidson, 2001). Such self-evaluation is especially important in schools that pilot unique educational innovations. Charter schools in particular are seen as research and development "laboratories" for testing innovations in education, innovations that, if proven successful, can be adopted by other schools. Without evidence that these educational innovations can produce the intended results, the charter school movement's potential as a mechanism for overall school reform is greatly diminished.

An excellent resource specific to internal evaluation of charter schools is C. Awsumb-Nelson's (2001) *Strengthening Your School's Accountability Plan: A Technical Assistance Manual for Cleveland Community Schools,* available at http://www.wmich.edu/evalctr/charter/cleveland/accountability_manual.pdf.

NOTE

1. For more information on NCLB, please see http://www.ed.gov.

2

Focusing the Evaluation

It is not sufficient to state that evaluation can and should be a part of all school improvement activities. If responsibilities for evaluation are to be made clear, if evaluation findings are to be used, and if activities contributing to the evaluation are to be coordinated, you need to identify the specific elements of the school system that are to be evaluated.

POSSIBLE FOCAL POINTS FOR EVALUATION

One school district created the following list of school functions that might be assessed or evaluated:[1]

1. *Program needs:* to establish program goals and objectives

2. *Individual needs:* to provide insights about the instructional needs of individual learners

3. *Resource allotment:* to provide guidance in setting priorities for budgeting

4. *Processes or strategies for providing services to learners:* to provide insights about how best to organize a school to facilitate learning
   a. *Curriculum design:* to provide insights about the quality of program planning and organization
   b. *Classroom processes:* to provide insights about the extent to which educational programs are being implemented

c. *Materials of instruction:* to provide insights about whether specific materials are indeed aiding student learning

d. *Monitoring of pupil progress:* to conduct formative (in-progress) evaluations of student learning

e. *Learning motivation:* to provide insights about the effort and persistence of learners

f. *Teacher effectiveness:* to provide insights about the effectiveness of teachers in aiding students to achieve goals and objectives of the school

g. *Learning environment:* to provide insights about the extent to which students are provided a responsive environment in terms of their educational needs

h. *Staff development:* to provide insights about the extent to which the school system provides the staff with opportunities to increase their effectiveness

i. *Decision making:* to provide insights about how well a school staff—principal, teachers, and others—make decisions that result in learner benefits

j. *Community involvement:* to determine the extent to which community members can aid in the decision-making process of the school

k. *Board policy formation:* to provide insights about the extent to which the board is using its authority to communicate its expectations to the staff

5. *Outcomes of instruction:* to provide insights about the extent to which students are achieving the goals and objectives set for them

GETTING STARTED

Where Does One Begin?

The evaluation of a school program usually begins when someone or some group (usually teachers) has a concern about the current program. The principal might initiate the evaluation and get a group of faculty members to take the lead. Or a grade-level or department committee could initiate the evaluation. However it starts, those doing the evaluation should plan to meet as a group to consider, as a first step, the following questions:

1. Why do you want to evaluate the program? What led to this decision? What is the purpose of the evaluation?

2. Who will use the results? How will they use them? Who else should be involved in the evaluation and see the results?

3. What is the program? What does it include? Exclude? Is it this year's program, last year's, or next year's that we will be evaluating? At what grade level? As implemented by which teachers? Is this the first time the program has been evaluated?

4. How much time and money do you have for the evaluation? Who is going to do it? Have you talked with others about the evaluation? Are they in support?

An important decision when planning an evaluation is whether to use internal or external evaluators. That decision should be based in part on the intended purpose of the evaluation. Evaluations can be conducted for *formative* purposes; that is, for further developing and improving the program, or *summative* purposes, such as major decisions regarding accountability and consequences. Generally, internal evaluations are conducted for formative purposes and summative evaluations are conducted by impartial outsiders.

Internal Evaluation/Formative Evaluation

An internal evaluation, which is conducted internally by staff who are working in the program, is usually *formative* in nature. Its purpose is to gather feedback on aspects of the program that are undergoing review and possible revision. What is working well and what is not? What needs fixing? Is there a need for midcourse corrections? The evaluation is generally not intended for outsiders; however, it can be shared with outsiders as a way of demonstrating that school staff are taking an active role in evaluating and improving their own school.

Whenever possible, internal staff will function most effectively for formative program evaluations because of their familiarity with the program context, including student needs and the school culture, and because of their ability to continue with their involvement in program change after the evaluation has been completed. That having been said, it is also advisable to have an external review of the formative program evaluation, called a metaevaluation, by independent external evaluators to address concerns about bias of internal evaluators.

External Evaluation/Summative Evaluation

Another type of evaluation, *external evaluation,* is conducted by staff who are outside the program's setting. It usually is motivated by questions from outside and requires accurate responses to questions that outsiders pose. External evaluations are often *summative:* decisions about replacements, major overhauls, awards, or other accountability decisions often are the end results. NCLB mandates are one form of external evaluation. Their purposes can be both formative in that they provide input on what areas need improving, and summative in that they can result in the profound restructuring of a school.

Because of the emphasis on accountability in summative program evaluation, external evaluators are most effective because of their independence and ability to step back to take an objective look at the big picture, which may include more than just looking at a school or school district. Community, state, and federal issues may come into play in a summative evaluation. External evaluators are often professional evaluation contractors.

GETTING SOME STRUCTURE FOR THE EVALUATION

After the questions listed in the above section have been answered, a decision should be made about proceeding with the evaluation. If it looks as if no one will use the results or the evaluation cannot be done well, you should question the logic of moving ahead.

When you do plan to move ahead with an evaluation, however, there are certain decisions that will need to be made. A discussion of each of these decisions follows.

Selecting a Coordinator

A basic decision is determining who will coordinate the evaluation. Important considerations are whether these people have the time, the program expertise and credibility, the concern or interest, and the leadership and organizational skills necessary to coordinate the evaluation. Select carefully, for this is a critical decision that should not be taken lightly.

Stakeholders

Once an evaluation group has emerged, decisions need to be made about who the evaluation is for. Typically, in-house evaluations are done for the staff who will be making changes to improve the program. On the other hand, one can ill afford to ignore certain groups or individuals. In an evaluation of a science program, for example, certainly all teachers who teach science should receive information about the evaluation and, often, should be asked to participate in it. The evaluation group may also want to involve interested parents and school board members, local community leaders and employers, or local educators with expertise in science education (e.g., someone from a university, someone from an intermediate school district, or the district science coordinator if your school district has one). Each individual or group who has an interest in the quality of the science program is called a *stakeholder*. These stakeholders have different perspectives and values when it comes to science education. Their values are worth considering seriously in an open evaluation process, and the results of evaluation could be shared with them if you think doing so would make a difference.

Holiday Headache: The Price of Excluding Key Stakeholders in an Evaluation

A small school district was trying to decide whether to adopt a particular elementary school social studies curriculum whose theme revolved around the celebration of holidays in various cultures. The district hired a team of curriculum experts, as well as authorities from various cultures and religions, to evaluate the curriculum on its accuracy and appropriateness for elementary school students.

The evaluation team conducted an extensive qualitative analysis of each unit of the curriculum. They found the curriculum developmentally appropriate for its intended students. They found the curriculum accurate for the most part, although they had a few suggestions for adapting it to make it more authentic. The school district decided to adopt the curriculum with the team's suggested adaptations.

Soon after the curriculum was implemented, the district began receiving complaints from principals and teachers, as well as irate phone calls and letters from parents. While some administrators and teachers were delighted with the exciting new curriculum, some complained that it took precious time away from learning the material needed for the state's standardized tests in social studies. A few teachers complained that the new curriculum interrupted the activities that they had already carefully mapped out the previous year. However, the most vocal opponents were parents from a wide variety of religious and political beliefs. A few parents complained that the curriculum watered down their sacred traditions into a frivolous, secularized party. Others were offended because their own particular cultures were excluded from the curriculum. Numerous other parents complained that the activities violated the principle of separation of church and state. After considerable pressure from parents, the district decided to pull the plug on the curriculum for the following year, much to the disappointment of the teachers, parents, and students who had been looking forward to it. Tensions among school staff ensued.

Clarifying What Is to Be Evaluated

Another set of decisions is needed to get a clear sense of what is to be evaluated. For example, the concept of "hands-on learning" in science has been touted as an essential part of science education. Closer inspection of what one means when the term *hands-on* is used, however, will reveal a wide variety of conceptions; only some of these have proven to be effective, whereas others have little educational value. One can only evaluate clear and accurate descriptions of whatever aspects of the program one has chosen to study. Aspects of a program being evaluated that should be clarified include the following:

- Which grade levels are involved?
- Which courses and teachers are involved?
- What is the basic organizational structure of the program? What are its major components and activities?

- How many students are involved at each grade level and for what amounts of time?
- What resources (human, materials, time) are consumed by the program?
- What is the curriculum design for the program (scope and sequence)?
- What needs are being served by the program?
- Have there been evaluations of the program in the past? If so, what did they find and recommend?

Describing What Is to Be Evaluated

The best way to get a clear idea of what is to be evaluated is to *observe* the program in action, talk to *(interview)* other staff, and *read* documents about the program (e.g., curriculum guides, lists of objectives). Once you have a clear sense of what is to be evaluated, it is a good idea to write it down so that others will know what you are talking about and so that you will have a record of the program as it once was in case it is changed while you are evaluating it. When changes occur, as they often do with programs, you will want to redescribe the program as it unfolds. These descriptions should be included in the final report.

To achieve clarity about a program, evaluators often make use of a *logic model* to describe the program. In Figure 2.1, a program logic model is used to describe the following components of the program:

Figure 2.1   A Program Logic Model

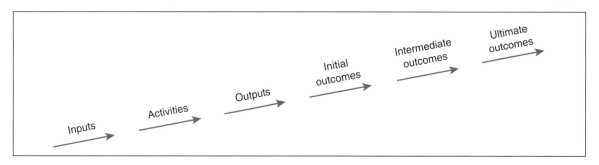

SOURCE: Reproduced from *Measuring Program Outcomes: A Practical Approach* (1996). Reprinted by permission, United Way of America.

- *Inputs* describe the resources (fiscal and human) needed to run the program, as well as facilities, equipment, books, materials, and other essential ingredients.
- *Activities* describe what you will be doing in the program—the scope and sequence of activities, a timeline, and assigned personnel who will be conducting the activities.
- *Outputs* describe the numbers associated with the program— numbers and demographics of students, number of contact hours, number of classroom and home assignments and time involved in

each, number and types of tests and work products, and student/ teacher ratio.

- *Initial outcomes* describe the expected student changes that will occur after each activity (e.g., each class). How should students be different from before the activity?
- *Intermediate outcomes* describe the expected longer-term student changes that will occur after a lengthy engagement in the program (e.g., at the end of a semester or year).
- *Ultimate outcomes* describe the vision you have for students who have successfully completed a program of study. This is the ideal. To what extent have they developed as you had hoped?

Successful program developers often start with the end—the ultimate outcomes or vision—and then work backward to design a program that will get students to that end. Outputs, intermediate outcomes, and initial outcomes become checkpoints or benchmarks so that progress toward the ultimate outcome can be assessed and midcourse changes can be made if needed. Activities and inputs can be planned as the *means* for reaching the intended initial, intermediate,

> For more information on developing logic models, please see W. K. Kellogg Foundation Logic Model Development Guide (2001), available online at http://www.wkkf.org/Pubs/Tools/ Evaluation/Pub3669.pdf.

and ultimate outcomes. A program designed in this way lends itself quite readily to an evaluation keyed to intended outcomes.

The early decisions that must be made are as follows:

- Who will do the evaluation?
- Who are the stakeholders in this evaluation?
- What is to be evaluated?
- What resources and personnel are available for the evaluation?

Availability of Resources

A final set of decisions relates to the resources and personnel available to the evaluation. The amount of money, time, support personnel, and existing data that are available will influence the complexity of the evaluation. You can do only so much with limited resources. You need to be realistic. Knowing the resources available to you will help you plan a feasible program evaluation.

After you have addressed these decisions, it will be time to develop a list of evaluation questions that will guide the program evaluation.

ILLUSTRATIVE CASE STUDY (PART 2)

In a faculty meeting at the beginning of the year, Ms. Goss announced that the science program would be evaluated during the year in order to get direction for improving it. The evaluation would be done by a science evaluation committee of interested teachers, with some outside help from graduate students in education from a nearby university. Any teachers who wanted to serve on the science evaluation committee were invited to volunteer, and the first meeting of the committee was scheduled to be held after school the next Monday. Six teachers volunteered; fortunately, they were evenly split among the grades.

Ms. Goss met with the science evaluation committee on the following Monday and reviewed the purpose of the evaluation. "Although we are concerned about the state test scores," she said, "there are several of us who also feel it is time to review and revamp our science program. It has been so long since it was systematically evaluated that none of us remembers when it was last done.

"Ms. Cooper has been a primary teacher in this school for 22 years, and the only evaluation she is aware of is what was done by the last textbook selection committee when it was asked to select a science textbook. Otherwise, each teacher has been doing her or his own thing! I'm not sure how much revamping the curriculum even changed that. We want to use the results of this evaluation to look at our science program and to see how well we fit with our current curriculum. Are we preparing our children to meet the demands of the science program in later grades?"

Ms. Goss continued. "Mr. Henry has been to two National Science Foundation workshops and has taken several summer science workshops at the college. He has also had a course in program evaluation as part of his master's degree. For these reasons, I have asked him to coordinate this evaluation. We have a little money to cover incidental expenses, but check with me before you spend anything. I expect the final report to be presented at a faculty meeting this spring, but I'll leave Mr. Henry in charge of scheduling the specifics. Does anyone have any questions before we break?"

Mr. Henry asked the committee to hold meetings on Mondays after school for the science evaluation study, at least for the month. The members all agreed and departed.

IDENTIFYING THE EVALUATION QUESTIONS

Evaluations answer questions about strengths and weaknesses of a program from a number of different perspectives. You can ask how good a school program is from the perspectives of key stakeholders such as the faculty, who teach in it; parents, who have certain expectations; or employers, who have to live with its products. You can also ask how good a program is according to how well it meets its objectives, how well its students perform on normed tests, or how well it matches a "model" program as defined by the profession (e.g., for science programs, the National Science Teachers Association [NSTA]) or professional literature (e.g., on effective schools or on what works, as published by the U.S. Department of Education). All of these are legitimate ways to evaluate a program, but they can result in different conclusions. To get the most informed look at a program, it is usually necessary to draw from a wide variety of approaches. It is important to be thorough, and the selection of the questions to address in the evaluation is the way to ensure a thorough program examination.

Figure 2.2   Evaluation Information Collection and Analysis Worksheet (Blank)

Evaluation Questions	Why the Question Is Important	Information Needed to Answer the Question	When and How the Information Will Be Collected	Data Analysis and Interpretation Procedures

Evaluation Worksheet

How is the selection of questions accomplished? Easy. Start with a blank worksheet like that presented in Figure 2.2. You are going to fill in the first and second columns (usually it will require several copies of the worksheet to list the most critical questions).

How to Identify Evaluation Questions

One venue is to talk to key stakeholders you have identified (teachers in the program and perhaps certain parents, employers, or a science consultant). If they were going to look at the science program, for instance, what are the most important things they would look for? What are the characteristics of a good science program from their perspective? How would they know a good one if they saw it? Ultimately, what is their vision of a student who has successfully completed the program? By keeping careful notes of their responses, you should have a good initial list of candidate questions for the evaluation. Of course, you will not be able to address every question thrown at you, but you should come up with a select list of questions that will be essential from the perspective of the stakeholders.

Teachers in the program may ask whether the text, curriculum materials, and lab exercises are up to date and consistent with state and NSTA guidelines.[2] Parents may ask what is expected of a student at the end of a grade level in terms of science knowledge, skills, and values. They may also want to know how well their children are being prepared for college, jobs, or national exams. A school board member may ask about the need for additional or fewer secondary-level courses and may be concerned about costs of the program. Stakeholders will help you to focus on the important questions.

You could also plan to compare your program against some existing model or ideal program. The characteristics of a model science program, for instance, could come from standards supplied by your state department of education, from the effective-schools literature, from NSTA, from the goals for the year 2061 established by the American Association for the Advancement of Science (AAAS), from the federal "what works" publications, from the evaluation criteria used for accreditation, or from certain lighthouse programs that have been identified as being exemplary. You could look at these sources and pull out the characteristics that your program should have. Use your fellow teachers and others who are key people to help you do this so that major stakeholders have a voice in the selection of evaluation questions.

Finally, you could plan to call in an outside program-area expert, if one is available to you, to indicate what an outside expert might look for in an exemplary program. Add what the expert tells you to the list of questions you have already started.

Narrowing Down the List of Questions

Next, the teachers doing the evaluation should meet to shorten the list of evaluation questions if it is too long to be workable. The logic model may be helpful here. For a complete evaluation, each step of the logic model should correspond with at least one evaluation question; however, it may not be feasible for an evaluation to cover every step of the logic model. The second column of Figure 2.2 will help—if you cannot explain why a particular evaluation question is also important, you have to wonder why it is even being addressed. Looking beyond the importance of the question, you can reduce the list by considering who would be upset if the question were dropped, whether the information already exists, and whether it is feasible to try to get an answer to the question.

Concentrate on the most critical questions for your program evaluation and then fill in the first two columns on the worksheet.

You have just finished focusing the evaluation. Basically, you have done the following:

- Clarified the evaluation purposes
- Clarified what is to be evaluated
- Identified the evaluation questions to be answered

ILLUSTRATIVE CASE STUDY (PART 3)

The next Monday found the science program evaluation committee meeting after school. Having read *Evaluating School Programs: An Educator's Guide,* the committee members understood the importance of getting multiple perspectives about what to look at in the science program.

Mr. Henry took a piece of paper out of his pocket. "Let's review two things at this meeting. First, let's make a list of who might have an interest in improving our science program, and then let's decide who will contact each group or individual to see what questions they would like us to address. We can then narrow down the questions to a reasonable list that will guide our work this year." After some discussion, it was decided that Ms. Radisson (Grades K–2) and Mr. Henry (Grades 3–5) would talk individually with each of the other teachers in the school to ask them what they would look at if they were asked to determine whether the science program at Lakeview Elementary School was a good one or a poor one. Ms. Chang, a fourth-grade teacher, volunteered to contact a school board member she knew to see if she could get a reading on school board interests.

Ms. Cooper agreed to get on the phone to the PTA. The PTA would be asked to contact at least 30 parents to determine their expectations, especially related to student outcomes. The list of parents was one Ms. Cooper would give them. The list represented a good cross section of grade levels of enrolled children and social classes of families; it was one that Ms. Goss had used on occasion to get parent input on school issues. Ms. Cooper would ask the PTA for the information by next week.

The following week, all committee members came to the meeting ready with their lists of evaluation questions. Mr. Henry typed out each question on his laptop, which was connected to an overhead projector, as it was read. He combined questions that were getting at the same thing. In total, 28 questions were listed.

Ms. Chang commented, "We have so many questions from so many stakeholders. How can we narrow them down?"

Mr. Henry explained, "Let's go back to the logic model. That will help sort out some of the most important questions. Then we'll go back and see where and if the other questions fit in." He opened a document with the logic model in Figure 2.1 on the computer, and the staff worked together to cut and paste the questions in the appropriate places on the logic model. They further pruned out questions that were redundant or irrelevant. Ultimately, it looked something like the model in Figure 2.3.

Figure 2.3   Evaluation Questions Arranged on Logic Model

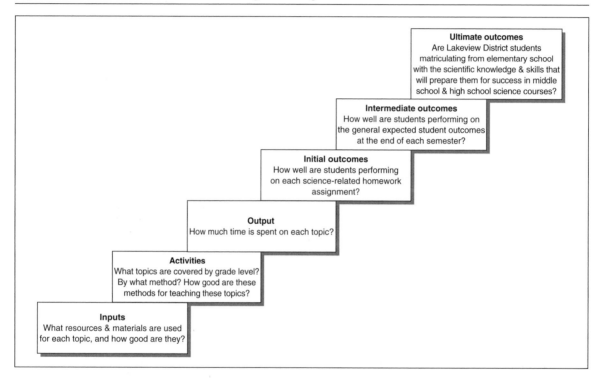

Ms. Chang gasped, "Do you expect us to get the answers to the ultimate outcomes by this spring?"

"Of course not," replied Mr. Henry. "We'll scratch that one off the list. But it's a good guiding question when we eventually ask ourselves what the intermediate outcomes should be."

Ms. Chang laughed. "Beyond NCLB, does anyone really know what our school's expected outcomes are? Or what they should be? Are they even aligned with our school's new curriculum? As someone mentioned earlier, all the teachers just seem to do their own things!"

Mr. Henry agreed. "Yes, several teachers have made that point earlier. I think it's worth further investigation." He added a corresponding question to the top of the list.

"And what about the question regarding each student's homework assignment?" questioned Ms. Radisson. "How could we possibly consolidate all that data into anything meaningful? It's apples and oranges, especially since each teacher is doing his or her own thing."

"Good point," said Mr. Henry. "We'll focus on the general outcomes for now and add a question about how well they are aligned with the curriculum."

Ms. Cooper asked, "But what about the appropriateness of the curriculum itself? I know we hired someone to help revamp it last year, but is it really in line with what our school needs as well as NCLB requirements?"

"One more excellent idea," Mr. Henry added. "We may need to tweak the curriculum once we get the results of the other answers. That will be our final question, but we might have to defer answering it until next year."

The committee then recombined and reordered some of the remaining questions to make them more feasible to proceed with data collection (see Figure 2.4). The rationales for asking each question were then listed in the second column of the table. Mr. Henry agreed to e-mail the list to Ms. Goss and all other teachers in the school with a note saying that these would be the questions the science evaluation study would address. Anyone who had a comment or reaction to the list was invited to e-mail the committee to discuss revising the list. Otherwise, the committee would go with the list as it was.

Figure 2.4   Evaluation Information Collection and Analysis Worksheet (First Two Columns Completed)

Evaluation Questions	Why the Question Is Important
1. Are the expected student outcomes of the science classes congruent with the school's overall science curriculum?	1. We need to agree upon appropriate outcomes that correspond with our vision for student development in science.
2. What topics are covered by grade level, and is sufficient time spent on each?	2. We need to know what we are doing to meet our goals.
3. What materials and methods are used for each topic, and how good are they?	3. We need to analyze our instruction to identify targets for improvement.
4. How well are students performing on the general expected outcomes?	4. We need to know how well we are meeting our goals. Are we progressing in such a way that it is likely that we will meet our ultimate student outcomes?
5. To what extent is the curriculum meeting our expectations?	5. We need to be clear about our standards and their appropriateness.

When the list and note were distributed, there were no complaints about the five questions that had emerged. However, a number of teachers added that a thorough evaluation should address concerns such as the low achievement of low-income students, the effects of discipline problems on teaching and learning, and the problem of uninvolved parents. A number of teachers complained vociferously about the NCLB mandates in general. One stated (hopefully facetiously) that the evaluation was a waste of time, since NCLB dictated that we should just teach to the test and get it over with.

A Note on the Case Study:
Moving From Gripe Sessions to Productivity

Several of the teachers' questions resembled the gripe session from the original meeting: How can we focus on science achievement alone when there are legitimate concerns about the effects of poverty, lack of parental support, and discipline problems? These problems impact not only standardized science test scores but the school as a whole! Sure, there were always professional development sessions designed to address these issues—did they ever really change anything or were they just window dressing? Mr. Henry couldn't let these issues go. At home, he brainstormed some responses to the complaints he heard from fellow staff—and the phenomena he witnessed among students—on a painfully frequent basis.

Our low-income students can't possibly live up to such high standards!

- What are the limitations of these students? What needs do they have?
- What can the school do to address these needs (e.g., referrals to community services, afterschool enrichment programs, tutoring)?
  – How well are the current services meeting these needs?
- Are low expectations of staff and peers part of the problem?

If their parents can't parent, we can't teach!

- How do parents perceive school staff? How are our school-parent communications? How can they be improved?
- Are we able to communicate with parents who have economic barriers? Linguistic barriers?
- How can we improve opportunities for parents to be directly involved in their children's education? In the school governance and decision making?
- Are there adequate staff available to address issues (or make referrals for such issues) such as child care, family dysfunction, child abuse/neglect, and so on?

If only we didn't have to deal with problem students . . .

- How pervasive, frequent, and severe are students' behavior problems? Have they been improving or getting worse over time?
- How effective are the school's discipline policies? What needs to be changed?
- What additional resources are needed to address behavior problems?
- Are classroom or school dynamics exacerbating problem behavior (e.g., teachers insidiously encouraging peers to scapegoat particular children)? If so, how can they be addressed?

I guess we have to scrap that new program, as promising as it seemed, and teach to the test instead . . .

- How much are the students learning from the new program?
- Does the new program effectively address issues that indirectly affect learning (e.g., improve student behavior, increase motivation to learn, decrease bullying, etc.)?
- Should we keep the program while finding additional ways to improve our test scores (e.g., incorporate lessons that correspond to areas that will be tested)?

The %$@%$ NCLB is a totally inappropriate way to evaluate OUR unique school!

- On the basis of our school's mission and related goals, what ARE important criteria to measure?
  - How can they best be measured?
  - What are the standards/benchmarks?
  - How can the results best be used?
    - If they contradict our NCLB scores, then what?
    - If they confirm the NCLB scores, then what?

Mr. Henry realized that the science evaluation committee could only address so much. Although discipline, parental involvement, and other student needs affected students' performance in science, it was necessary to limit the scope of the evaluation to the effectiveness of the current science curriculum.

The other issues he presented to Ms. Goss, who in turn presented them to the PTA and the newly formed discipline committee. She realized that both groups were continuously trying the latest programs or policies in attempts to improve matters. However, neither group had ever done any evaluations of these efforts beyond simple satisfaction surveys, which never gave much useful information. If the science evaluation committee was successful in conducting a useful evaluation to guide the improvement process, perhaps the PTA and the discipline committee could be inspired to do likewise.

NOTES

1. The terms *assessment* and *evaluation* are often used interchangeably. However, evaluation is more comprehensive and broader in scope. Assessments of particular variables are often crucial components of an in-depth evaluation. For example, a standardized test is an assessment of student learning in a particular area, which is one aspect of evaluating a school's quality and effectiveness.

2. See http://www.nsta.org.

3

Collecting
Information

To complete Columns 3 and 4 in the evaluation worksheet (see Figure 2.2), you will have to identify the information you need to answer each question and then specify when and how the information will be collected. These two columns provide a structure for the methods that will be used to conduct the evaluation.

INFORMATION NEEDS AND SOURCES

For each question in the first column of the worksheet, one must ask what information is needed to answer the question. Usually, the response is fairly straightforward. For example, if the question is, How well are students performing on science objectives? the information needed to answer the question might be scores on teacher-made unit tests, results on a state assessment test, or results of portfolios graded with a rubric. But the answer might also include results on performance assessments in which, for example, students might have a chance to solve problems or make decisions while working on a science project. Other important questions might be answered using a career-interest inventory or an "attitudes toward science" questionnaire.

Where to get the information is also an important consideration. You should use data already in existence whenever possible. This will save a lot of time and money, which are usually in short supply in schools. If the information is not readily available, then you need to think about who or where the best information source will be. Here is a list of common sources of information in school program evaluation:

- Students
- Teachers
- Principals or program directors
- School board members
- State education department staff
- Parents
- University specialists
- Direct observation of the program
- Libraries, the Internet, and other sources of public documents
- School files and records
- Professional associations

If the source of critical information is not evident, it is permissible and simple enough to ask others for suggestions about where you might best obtain such information. This is also a good way to involve stakeholders in the evaluation. Also, keep in mind that you can only do what is feasible. In many cases of internal evaluation, informal discussions and other less formal methods might be appropriate.

IDENTIFYING METHODS AND INSTRUMENTS FOR COLLECTING INFORMATION

The methods that evaluators use to collect information change with every evaluation. There often is no single method or instrument that can satisfy the information needs of all questions that might be asked. Consequently, evaluators must carry with them a toolbox of alternative methods and instruments to draw from as the need arises. What follows is a listing of common formal methods and instruments used to gather information in program evaluation. A book could be written about how to develop and use each method (and such books have been written), but a detailed or technical discussion goes beyond what is possible in this guide and is not the intent here. This section of the guide provides a list of alternative ways that may be used to collect information. The details are left up to the many excellent and already existing references that are cited. With each method is a reference list of one or more other sources in case more detail is needed about any particular method or instrument.

Often, informal methods of data collection such as group discussions, informal observations, and reflections of key informants will also be appropriate for school program evaluations. Do not overlook any sources of information when you are conducting an evaluation. You want the best evidence available to guide you when you are making decisions.

Testing

Testing is by far the most common method of collecting information from and about students in education. In testing for student achievement, there are two major categories of tests: (1) norm-referenced tests and (2) criterion-referenced tests.

Norm-Referenced Testing

Norm-referenced tests compare a student's performance on a broad range of skills and knowledge against those of other students who took the same test. The administration procedures are standardized. Examples include the Iowa Tests of Basic Skills, the Iowa Tests of Educational Development, the Stanford Achievement Test, the Metropolitan Achievement Test, the California Achievement Test, and the Comprehensive Test of Basic Skills.

Criterion-Referenced Testing

Criterion-referenced tests assess a student's performance on a domain of skills or on a set of instructional objectives or standards. Examples include textbook unit tests, teacher-made tests, basic skills competency tests, and performance tests. Criterion-referenced tests are used most commonly in internal program evaluations by school personnel. In recent years, schools have begun assembling portfolios of different kinds of evidence of what a student can do. By using a wide range of student assessments, educators believe they can get a better picture of a student's abilities and achievements than they can by using one multiple-choice, paper-and-pencil test.

Standards governing the use of tests are available and are a must reading for anyone using tests with students. These standards include *Standards for Teacher Competence in Educational Assessment of Students, Code of Fair Testing Practices in Education, Code of Professional Responsibilities in Educational Measurement,* and *Standards for Educational and Psychological Testing.* Information about obtaining copies of these documents is available from the National Council on Measurement in Education, 1230 17th Street N.W., Washington, DC 20036 (see also http://www.ncme.org).

Guidelines for Testing

If you are going to develop a test, some guidelines for writing good tests include the following:

- Be sure to be clear about what it is you want to measure.
- Develop a blueprint for the test that lists the topics to be covered in your content domain and the category of your objectives in Bloom's taxonomy (Bloom, Englehart, Furst, Hill, & Krathwohl, 1956; see also Resource C).
- Select the item formats to fit the kind of behavior you want demonstrated by your students, as well as the feasibility to score the tests. See Table 3.1 for a brief summary of item formats and their strengths and weaknesses.

Table 3.1   Formats of tests, uses, and complexity of scoring

Format	Uses	Complexity of Scoring
Essay tests	Organizing thoughts, writing skills, and synthesis of knowledge	High
True-false and multiple-choice items	Recall and application of responses	Very low
Short-answer and completion items	Recall and application of responses	Low
Matching items	Recognition of correct responses; examining relationships	Low

Regardless of the format used,

- Use clear directions.
- Allow enough time for completion.
- Keep the reading difficulty of the test items appropriate to what is being measured.

On true-false, multiple-choice, and matching items,

- Be careful that one test item does not give a clue for answering another.
- Avoid ambiguity.
- Avoid trivia.
- Beware of "specific determiners" such as *never* and *always*.
- Beware of giving clues to the correct answer through the length of the response choice.
- Be sure there is only one correct or clearly best answer.
- Develop more items than you need, pilot-test them, and select the best.

Examples of essay, true-false, multiple-choice, short-answer and completion, and matching test items are shown below.

Sample Essay Test Items

1. Surveys and tests are common methods for collecting information in program evaluation. Distinguish between the two methods by indicating how they are the same and how they are different. Indicate when you would use each.

2. Identify two sources of information that you would use to help design a survey study and two sources of information that you

would use to help develop a test. Give a summary of the information each source will provide.

3. Attached is a report of a survey study. Read the report and then indicate whether the study is good or bad. Give your reasons for your judgment and cite specific parts of the study to support your reasons.

Sample True-False Test Items

1. A blueprint for a test lists the format for the items to be included on the test.
   True   False

2. True-false items are used to assess writing skills.
   True   False

3. True-false test items can cover a relatively wide range of topics in a short span of time.
   True   False

Sample Multiple-Choice Test Items

1. In program evaluation, information collection follows
   a. Focusing the evaluation
   b. Analyzing information
   c. Reporting information
   d. Evaluating the evaluation

2. Follow-ups are conducted in surveys when
   a. The response rate is 100%
   b. There is a large number of nonrespondents
   c. A question was left off the questionnaire
   d. The questionnaires are lost

3. An example of a criterion-reference test is
   a. The Stanford Achievement Test
   b. The Iowa Test of Basic Skills
   c. The Metropolitan Achievement Test
   d. A teacher-made test

Sample Short-Answer and Completion Test Items

1. Two test item formats that are used to collect information about student recall of knowledge are _____ and _____.

2. Define norm-referenced testing: (short answer)

3. When are surveys used for information collections? (short answer)

Sample Matching Test Items

For each test item format in the list on the left, select the *best* use of that format from the list on the right.

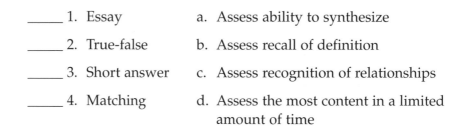

Notice how the reading difficulty in each of these examples is kept as simple as possible. The examples are clear and to the point, covering important topics. The multiple-choice items avoid the use of *never, always, all of the above,* and *none of the above.* Finally, each item has one best answer.

Your school district could benefit from starting a test or item file for each school subject. You could start by collecting tests and test items used by your teachers and then asking neighboring districts to share theirs. Eventually, you could build your collection by soliciting tests and items from all school districts in the state.

For more details about testing, you should find Airasian (1997) and Hopkins (1998) helpful.

In addition, commercially available tests are listed in *Tests in Print* and reviewed in the *Mental Measurements Yearbooks* published by the Buros Institute at the University of Nebraska. Test collections are available from the Educational Testing Service, Princeton, New Jersey, at http://www.ets.org.

Student Portfolios

A student portfolio is a purposeful collection of a variety of teacher observations and/or student products (e.g., reports, illustrations, project documentation, etc). The contents are systematically collected over time, as they are all reflective of progress toward particular goals. Often portfolios are assessed with detailed rubrics. A rubric is "a set of rules, guidelines, or benchmarks at different levels of performance" (Wheeler, Haertel, & Scriven, 1992).

For more information about portfolio assessment, please see Banta (2004).

Questionnaires/Surveys

Questionnaires and surveys (the terms are often used interchangeably) are collections of standard questions about a few issues placed on a form for response. Many questionnaires are developed locally, because the issues are idiosyncratic. Questionnaires can be done through the mail, over the Internet, or with intact groups (e.g., with a form that is distributed at a meeting or in a classroom). Follow-ups should be used with nonrespondents in mail and Internet surveys.

When developing a questionnaire, it is always wise to pilot-test it by asking people who are similar to the participants to attempt to complete it. They can usually tell you about confusing directions and unclear questions.

Some Guidelines for Questionnaires

Some guidelines for developing a questionnaire include the following:

- Provide clear instructions, including a due date.
- Do not ask leading questions.
- Group questions according to topic.
- Make it attractive.
- Keep it short.
- Do not assume too much knowledge.
- Begin by asking easy, impersonal questions.
- Do not ask double questions (i.e., two questions in one).
- State questions precisely.

An example of a questionnaire follows.

Sample Questionnaire

Please answer each of the following questions according to your best judgment or knowledge. There are no right or wrong answers, and your name will not be associated with your responses. All responses will be aggregated and reported for the total faculty. Please return this questionnaire by May 1.

1. In general, how would you rate the science resource room as a facility for providing necessary science instruction to your students?

    _____ Excellent, no problems

    _____ Good, a few problems

    _____ Average, several problems

    _____ Poor, many problems

    _____ Awful, filled with problems

There are a number of online survey programs available; some have free trial versions. Some of the most popular include

http://www.surveymonkey.com

http://www.zoomerang.com

http://www.questionpro.com

http://www.hostedsurvey.com

However, for short, simple surveys, such sophisticated programming is often unnecessary. Avoid creating lengthy, unwieldy surveys that are unlikely to be completed, just because the software is available to facilitate it!

2. How often do you use the science resource room per month on average?

     _____ Not at all

     _____ 1–2 times

     _____ 3–4 times

     _____ 5–6 times

     _____ 7–8 times

     _____ More than 8 times

3a. Are the facilities of the science resource room adequate?

     Yes   No

3b. If no, what is needed?

4a. Do you have problems getting access to the science resource room?

     Yes   No

4b. If yes, please describe the problem.

5a. Was your orientation to the science resource room adequate?

     Yes   No

5b. If no, what is needed?

6. What can be done to improve the science resource room?

Notice how the questions are kept short and to the point. The instructions are clear and the questions are stated precisely. No double questions are asked, and questions are worded so that they do not lead the respondent to answer in a certain way.

For more details about developing questionnaires, you should find the following sources useful: Dillman (2000), Fink (2005), and Gall, Borg, & Gall (1996).

Interviews

Interviews are used to deliver questions and record responses when a personal contact is needed to boost the rate of response, to probe beyond initial responses, or to get a fast response. Interviewers need to be trained because their personal behaviors and appearance can affect the responses they receive. They are a critical part of the interview process.

There are many recording devices for interviews, but they are not always necessary. Carefully taken notes may suffice and are less expensive and time consuming than transcriptions. An interviewer should give the interviewee a choice as to whether he or she wants the interview recorded.

Guidelines for Interviews

Some guidelines for an interview protocol (the questionnaire used by interviewers) include the following:

- Keep the language pitched to the level of the respondent.
- Clearly explain the purpose of the interview, who has access to the recordings or transcripts, and how it will be kept confidential.
- Encourage honesty, but let people know they can refuse to answer a question if they choose.
- Establish rapport by asking easy, impersonal questions first.
- Avoid long questions.
- Avoid ambiguous wording.
- Avoid leading questions.
- Limit questions to a single idea.
- Do not assume too much knowledge.

An example of an interview schedule follows.

Sample Interview Schedule

The questions I am about to ask you concern our science resource materials. Please be frank when responding. Your name will not be associated with your responses. We will compile all faculty responses into an aggregated report.

1. First, we want to know how you are using the materials. In what ways are you using them?

   Probe questions:
   a. What ways of using these materials have you found especially satisfactory? Why do you think these ways have been so satisfactory?
   b. Have you tried some things you won't try again? What are they? Why wouldn't you use them again?
   c. Which materials have you used? Why did you select these materials?

2. Next, we want to learn whether the use of the science materials has made any difference in your students' achievements. Has the use of the science materials resulted in student achievement?

   Probe questions:
   a. What difference has it made? Which materials made a difference?
   b. Do the materials cause you to spend more time on certain topics? Which topics?
   c. Do all students benefit? Which ones do or do not? Why?

Notice that the questions are clear and worded in an easy style. Each set of questions covers a single topic. The questions are not leading but do probe into details about the response given by the interviewee.

For more details about developing interview protocol, you should find Fowler & Mangione (1990) and Gall et al. (1996) helpful.

Attitude Scales

Attitudes are predispositions toward some group, institution, or abstract concept. This is one area of collecting information in which it is advised that you select from existing instruments, such as collections of attitude scales, rather than constructing your own. Fortunately, there are many such instruments available. If the available scales do not hit your target exactly, you can modify the wording of the scales, keeping the format intact, without causing too much damage to the original purpose of the instrument.

An example of a Likert-type attitude scale follows.

Sample Attitude Scale

SA = Strongly Agree

A = Agree

U = Undecided

D = Disagree

SD = Strongly Disagree

Circle the response that best fits your feelings. There are no right or wrong answers. Your name will not be associated with your response.

1. Science is my favorite subject.	SA A U D SD
2. I feel especially capable when studying science.	SA A U D SD
3. It is easy to get good marks in science.	SA A U D SD
4. Science exercises often scare me.	SA A U D SD
5. Science requires too much of my time.	SA A U D SD
6. Science is very useful in life.	SA A U D SD
7. What we are asked to do in science is just too much.	SA A U D SD
8. Science often makes my mind go blank.	SA A U D SD
9. More school time should be given to science.	SA A U D SD
10. I enjoy reading science books in my spare time.	SA A U D SD

Notice that each statement addresses some aspect of feelings about the topic, science. The statements are clearly worded, short, and to the point. The statements are a mixture of positive and negative attitudes. The directions provide guidance in how to respond.

Sources of attitude scales include Robinson, Shaver, & Wrightsman (1991).

Commercially available attitude instruments may also be found in *Tests in Print* and the *Mental Measurements Yearbooks* published by the Buros Institute at the University of Nebraska.

Observation Checklists

Observation checklists can be selected from existing instruments, or they can be developed locally. If you are going to take an inventory of whether certain conditions exist in your school or classroom, you can simply compile the list of desirable characteristics and then check.

An example of an observation checklist follows.

Sample Observation Checklist

Check those items that you see in evidence in the classroom you visit.

_____ Aquarium

_____ Science-related bulletin board

_____ Science posters on the wall

_____ Science resource books

_____ Science laboratory equipment

_____ Computers (list software _____)

_____ Other electronic materials (e.g., leap pads) (list_____)

_____ Live animals

_____ Bird feeder

_____ Scientific measurement instruments

_____ Other science-related materials (list _____)

Notice that the checklist provides a clear set of directions about how to respond. All items on the checklist are things that are clearly observable and evidence of science activity in the classroom. The checklist should be as comprehensive (i.e., exhaustive of indicators of science activities) as possible.

Unobtrusive Measures

Unobtrusive measures are methods for collecting information without affecting the natural behaviors of those who are being studied. You simply gather evidence without anyone being aware that it is happening. Consequently, unobtrusive (or nonreactive) measures often capture human behavior in its natural or typical form rather than in a contrived or peak-performance form. Another way of looking at unobtrusive measures is that you need to get creative when other forms of collecting information will not work or are not feasible. You need to ask yourself, "How will I know if I see it?" (referring to the behavior you want to measure), and then find ways to collect appropriate information. Unobtrusive measures can be informal observations: worn carpets in a certain location, worn books, actual use (consumption) of materials, archival records (e.g., library check-outs), newspaper or other mass media archival files, minutes, listening to informal conversations (and taking notes), absences, assignments, projects, grades, performances, and noting physical locations of people or objects. Basically, unobtrusive measures consist of *physical traces, archives,* and *observations.* The updated classic source on unobtrusive measures is Webb, Campbell, Schwartz, & Sechrest (2000).

Document analysis is used to summarize the content of a document or even a series of similar documents (so that trends can be noted over time). For example, by analyzing minutes of meetings or newspaper coverage on a topic of interest, the evaluator may find both the number of times a topic was covered and whether the discussion was positive or negative, as well as what changes were being discussed or recommended. This is a good way to get a sense of community feeling concerning a program, especially if it is a controversial one.

For more details on content analysis, you should find Weber (1990) helpful.

The formal methods and instruments listed above are commonly used in program evaluations. It would be a good idea to begin building a professional library at your school that includes the reference sources cited with each method or type of instrument and also to include existing instruments that you can keep on file and modify as needed for a particular program evaluation. Please keep in mind, however, that informal ways of gathering information are perfectly acceptable when formal data collection is simply not feasible.

Validity and Reliability

Two concepts to keep in mind when selecting a method or instrument for collecting information are *validity* and *reliability.* Validity is concerned with whether the instrument or method hits the target in providing you with the information you need. For example, many commercially available tests or off-the-shelf instruments would not cover the topics and objectives of Lakeview Elementary School's science program. They lack validity for that purpose. In *Statistics: A Spectator Sport* (1990), Richard Jaeger points out,

> When we collect data on a person for the purpose of research in education or the social sciences, we usually measure or observe *a sample* of that person's behavior. We might provide the person with a task to be completed or some set of stimulus materials that require a response. A traditional pencil-and-paper test is a good example. Alternatively, we might just observe the person in some naturally occurring situation, and count the incidences of some behavior or action. In recent years, much educational research has included observations of the incidence of specified students' or teachers' behaviors in classrooms. For example, a researcher might count the number of times, in a 15-minute period, that a teacher asks his or her students a direct question.
>
> If research merely involved reporting the number of test items a person answered correctly, or the number of times a teacher asked his or her students a question, there would be few validity issues. Validity concerns arise because researchers interpret these observable behaviors as indicators of a person's status on more general constructs such as "ability" or "interest." By generalizing beyond observed behaviors that occur at a particular time and in a particular setting, researchers and evaluators create a multitude of validity issues. The most fundamental concern is the appropriateness of the interpretations of the results of measurement. Measurement procedures are not *inherently* valid, nor inherently invalid. It is the *interpretations* of measurement results that must be examined for validity. (pp. 79–80)

There are four types of evidence that are frequently used to indicate measurement validity. As Jaeger (1990) tells us, they are

1. *Construct validity,* which is concerned with the total relationship between the results of a particular measurement and the underlying construct the evaluator is attempting to measure.

2. *Concurrent validity,* which is the correlation between an accepted measure of some construct and a new, yet unvalidated measure when they are taken at approximately the same time.

3. *Predictive validity,* which is the correlation between a measure used to predict some future performance and the measure used to indicate future performance.

4. *Content validity,* which is the degree to which the content of an instrument is representative of a larger domain of tasks or questions to which we want to generalize. There is no statistical evidence of content validity; it involves judging the content of an instrument.

Often, evaluators will use a blueprint or table of specifications to show how many questions on an instrument are used to measure each issue or type of behavior they want to assess.

Reliability

Reliability is concerned with error of measurement and whether the instrument or method is giving you a stable reading. On the topic of reliability, Jaeger (1990) writes,

It is well known that no measurement procedure—whether it is the use of a bathroom scale or the administration of an achievement test—is perfectly consistent. If you were to step on and off your bathroom scale five times in a row, chances are you would observe three or four different measurements of your weight. Depending on whether you placed your feet in exactly the same spot on the scale, and on the quality of the scale itself, the scale's indication of your weight might fluctuate by three or four pounds across the five measurements. The more consistent the indications of your weight, the more reliable is your bathroom scale. If the scale were to indicate exactly the same weight for you every time you stepped on and off (a highly unlikely occurrence), it would be totally consistent. We would then say that it was perfectly "reliable" *even though it might indicate the wrong weight every time* and thus give you an invalid weight. (In the *everyday* sense of "reliable" we would include validity, too; but in the technical sense, validity is a completely separate issue.)

When you observe the weight indicated by your bathroom scale, you are reading what measurement theorists call an *observed score*. This observed score can be thought of as consisting of two parts: one is your true weight (the *true score),* and the other is the results of a variety of factors that have nothing to do with your true weight (the *error component).* These other factors might include such things as the particular position of your feet on the scale (step too far forward, and the scale might read low; step too far backward and it might read high); the fact that you placed the scale on a thick rug instead of on the floor; and the tendency of the scale's springs to fatigue and recover depending on the rates at which you climb on and off the scale. In every measurement procedure, regardless of what is being measured or how it is being measured, the observed score that results from taking a measurement is equal to the sum of the true score and the error component. The reliability of the measurement procedure depends on the relative sizes of the true score and the error component. The larger the error component, the lower the reliability; the smaller the error component, the higher the reliability.

Measurement reliability is usually expressed as an index that can take on values between 0 and 1, much like a correlation coefficient. Unlike a correlation coefficient, though, the reliability of a measurement procedure can never be a negative number. A reliability of 0 means that the observed scores consist entirely of error components. A reliability of 1 would mean that the observed scores consist entirely of true scores; in reality, however, observed scores are composed of both true scores and error components, and their reliabilities are less than 1. (pp. 85–86)

Many available instruments have reliability coefficients reported with them. Several methods can be used to assess reliability when it is unknown. One method, called the *test-retest* method, involves giving an instrument to the same group of people twice and then calculating the correlation between the two sets of scores. Reliability estimation methods that require an instrument to be administered only once are called *internal consistency* methods. They indicate to what degree all of the measurements used in a procedure assess the same construct. Split-half, odd-even, Kuder-Richardson, and Cronbach's alpha are all different approaches to internal consistency reliability estimation.

Reliability is a concern as well when informal data collection methods are used. For example, informal conversations, a form of unobtrusive measurement, can change in tone from one day to the next. In cases when you are using unobtrusive measures or other informal methods with suspect reliability, you should back up your information by going to several sources (e.g., documents in the files or survey results) to confirm what your unobtrusive measurements are telling you. This is called *triangulating*, because you are usually basing your decisions on three or more different sources, rather than just one. Professional news reporters often use this strategy as a means of achieving accurate reporting.

Who Will Collect Information and When?

The final piece of planning to go into the collection of information is deciding who will collect the information and when they will do it. Normally, the job of collecting information will fall to the group that is doing the evaluation. There are many times, however, when the evaluators must ask others to help administer a test or a questionnaire. Therefore, it is important to plan ahead to specify who will collect the information, under what conditions, and when. This information can be recorded in the fourth column of the worksheet as shown in Table 3.2. A time schedule can then be made up for collecting data to answer each evaluation question; it will be important to talk to each person who will be participating to get everyone's cooperation and support. A follow-up memo to confirm dates and responsibilities can then be sent.

Timing

The timing of information collection is an important consideration. First, keep in mind when the evaluation is to be completed and then work backward. Second, consider when the information is going to be available.

Table 3.2 Evaluation Information Collection and Analysis Worksheet
(First Four Columns Completed)

Evaluation Questions	Why the Question Is Important	Information Needed to Answer the Question	When and How the Information Will Be Collected
1. Are the expected student outcomes of the science classes congruent with the school's overall science curriculum?	1. We need to have common goals and to be clear about our vision for student development in science.	1. What each teacher of science expects; what our curriculum guides say	1. In September, each teacher of science will be asked to list the 10 most important outcomes for students in science this year. These will be compared to the curriculum.
2. What topics are covered by grade level? Is sufficient time spent on each?	2. We need to know what we are doing to meet our goals.	2. Outlines of lesson plans from each teacher	2. In September, each science teacher will be asked to give his or her outlines of topics and time allocations to the evaluation coordinator.
3. What methods and materials are used for each topic, and how good are they?	3. We need to analyze our instruction to identify targets for improvement.	3. What each teacher uses; teachers' judgments of strengths and weaknesses of methods and materials	3. In January, each science teacher will be asked to list methods and materials for each topic and to evaluate each.
4. How well are students performing on the expected outcomes?	4. We need to know how well we are meeting our goals. Are we progressing in such a way that we will meet our ultimate student outcomes?	4. Various assessments of achievement of students in science	4. In February, each science teacher will be asked to list strong and weak outcomes of his or her students. In March–April, standardized science achievement scores and state assessment science scores will be compiled.
5. To what extent is the curriculum meeting our expectations?	5. We need to be clear about our standards and the extent to which we are meeting them.	5. The feasibility of applying the curriculum in the school; the integration of school-based goals and state-mandated content standards; the areas that need the most improvement according to earlier evaluation steps	5. Starting September of the following year, the science evaluation committee will review the curriculum in light of the data from earlier evaluation steps.

When is the most appropriate time to be collecting this information? Finally, consider when the information can be conveniently collected. Certain times of the year—the beginning and ending of the school year, summers, holidays, exam periods—are not good times to be collecting information in schools. Consider class times, lunchtimes, recesses, special events, and teacher preferences in developing the schedules. Being educators, the evaluators have to be sensitive to the needs of others in the school.

When collecting information, keep in mind certain issues that will need to be addressed. These are very practical points that can greatly affect the quality of the evaluation.

Practical Pointers for Collecting Information

Regardless of the specific data collection methods that you use, to collect adequate amounts of accurate data you will need sufficient buy-in from the participating stakeholders. Otherwise, crucial stakeholders will not be motivated to participate in the evaluation. You will also need accurate procedures for collecting, inputting, and storing the information. However, each of these phenomena have various barriers that require your careful attention.

1. **Participant buy-in.** What do you do when you run into problems of noncooperation or people not taking the data collection seriously?
   - To avoid such problems, you should explain the evaluation and its importance fully to participants and obtain their support prior to the beginning of the evaluation.
   - Choose methods that do not require an inordinate amount of time or effort. Surveys should be kept brief—rarely more than one or two pages. If lengthy processes such as interviews are necessary, some form of payback (e.g., released time, lunch) may help.
   - Staff may assume that an evaluation of an overall school program or project is really a personnel evaluation of their own work. Take the time to explain, orally and in writing, the purposes and scope of the evaluation.
   - Stakeholders may be concerned that the information they provide may be used against them (e.g., principals may insidiously punish teachers who criticize their work). Explicit assurance of confidentiality of questionnaires or interviews may alleviate concerns.
   - Conduct evaluation activities during times that are convenient for the stakeholders. Arrange for time to take a survey during staff meetings, rather than stuff a survey into their already overflowing mailboxes or e-mail boxes.
   - Choose a pleasant environment for data collection if the session is going to take a while. Good lighting and ventilation, comfortable seating, adequate spacing for group testing, and adequate monitoring for group testing are all recommended.
   - If problems occur during the evaluation, a private talk may help to show it is in everyone's best interest to participate.

- Follow up with a formal thank-you to any participants who went out of their way to provide information or to assist in the evaluation.

2. **Accuracy in data collection.** Buy-in issues notwithstanding, it is important to be on the lookout for potential problems in accurate data collection and to deal with them immediately when they appear. Better yet, proactively avoid such pitfalls. Table 3.3 outlines some of these potential problems and how to avoid them.

Table 3.3   What Can Go Wrong and How to Avoid It

What Can Go Wrong?	*Proactively Avoiding These Problems*
Respondents misunderstand directions and consequently respond inappropriately.	Pilot-test your methods.
Inexperienced data collectors make serious mistakes.	Train your data collectors and conduct trial runs.
Information gets lost.	Establish a rule that no original data leave the office; duplicate data and computer files; keep original data under lock and key.
Information is recorded incorrectly.	Build in cross-checks of recorded information.

To review, the collection of information involves the following:

1. Identifying sources of information for each evaluation question

2. Selecting evaluation methods that are appropriate for the evaluation questions being asked

3. Scheduling the collection of information

4. Assigning the tasks of collecting information to evaluation staff

ILLUSTRATIVE CASE STUDY (PART 4)

The science evaluation committee for the science program evaluation at Lakeview Elementary School met for its regular Monday afternoon planning meeting to formulate plans for addressing the questions it had selected for the evaluation. Three local graduate students in education, who were assisting with the evaluation as part of their internships, attended the meeting as well.

Mr. Henry began the meeting. "OK, it's time now to develop our plan for addressing the five questions and scheduling our work for the year. Let's begin. First, let's take each question and think about where we should go to get an accurate answer to the question. If we can go to several different sources, let's consider the easiest, most accessible source as the one we'll use. If we have some doubts about the accuracy of the information we'll get, we can go to two or three sources to make us feel better about the information we'll be basing our conclusions on. Let's start with Question 1."

The interns agreed to help Mr. Henry and the rest of the committee compare the teachers' stated outcomes with those of the curriculum. Question 2 was even easier. The teachers were already required to explicate their topics and the time spent on each in their outlines of lesson plans for each year, so there was no need to ask for additional information. The interns agreed to do some library work and online searches for characteristics of good elementary science instruction. They would also ask the director of the science education center at the university for copies of publications on what works in science education.

After considerable discussion on each question, the committee arrived at the plans recorded in Table 3.2. The members agreed to split up the task of going to the science teachers and sharing the plan with them, asking for reactions and agreement to participate as planned. Each committee member took responsibility for contacting the other teachers at one grade level in Lakeview Elementary. At a subsequent meeting, they were pleased to find out that they would get full cooperation.

The science evaluation committee also worked on the specifics of collecting information. Who was going to collect what and when? Ms. Chang stated, "If you think I'm going to do all of this, you're crazy. I've got enough to do being a good teacher. Besides, I've got a family, and I need to spend time with them!"

"I anticipated this problem," said Mr. Henry. "You are absolutely right that none of us has time to do what is necessary to carry this off. I talked to Ms. Goss about this issue, and she agreed to cover my class as needed to release me to coordinate the evaluation. We also have the three graduate students in education who will help with many of the time-consuming tasks. I will carry the ball, keep you informed, and then involve you at critical points, primarily in writing our report." There was a great sigh of relief in unison from five teachers. Mr. Henry smiled. "Now, let's work on specifics."

The work plan that the committee developed is presented in Table 3.4. Mr. Henry took this plan to Ms. Goss and got her approval, and then he distributed it to the other teachers in the school with a cover memo explaining his role as evaluation coordinator. Everyone was fully informed and ready to participate.

You are now ready to prepare a plan for organizing and analyzing program evaluation.

Table 3.4 Evaluation Work Plan

Evaluation Questions	Tasks	Task Beginning and End Date	Personnel Involved	Other Resources Needed and Costs
SCHOOL YEAR 1 1. Are the expected student outcomes of the science classes congruent with the school's overall science curriculum?	a. Create teacher survey forms b. Survey teachers c. Compile results d. Compare to curriculum e. Prepare report of strengths and weaknesses	a. Sept 1–15 (Year 1) b. Sept 15–30 c. Oct 1–15 d. Oct 15–30 e. Nov 1–15	a. Evaluation coordinator b. Evaluation coordinator c. Evaluation coordinator d & e. Evaluation coordinator; interns; science eval committee	Duplication of forms and reports: $20 Miscellaneous materials: $25
2. What topics are covered by grade level? Is sufficient time spent on each?	a. Lit review on best practices in instruction b. Collect outlines of lesson plans from teachers c. Compare lesson plans to best practices and to curriculum d. Prepare preliminary report of strengths and weaknesses e. Share with science teachers for feedback f. Revise report	a. Sept 1–30 (Year 1) b. Sept 15–30 c. Oct 1–30 d. Nov 1–15 e. Nov 15–30 f. Dec 1–20	a. Interns b. Evaluation coordinator c. Interns d. Interns; eval coordinator e. Evaluation coordinator f. Evaluation coordinator; science evaluation committee	Duplication of lesson plans and reports: $50
3. What methods and materials are used for each topic, and how good are they?	a. Create teacher survey form b. Survey teachers c. Compile results d. Review of findings e. Prepare report of strengths and weaknesses	a. Jan 3–15 (Year 1) b. Jan 15–Jan 30 c. Feb 1–Feb 15 d. Feb 15–Feb 28 e. Mar 1–Mar 30	a. Evaluation coordinator b. Evaluation coordinator c. Science eval committee; interns d. Science eval committee; interns	Duplication of forms and reports: $20
4. How well are students performing on the expected outcomes?	a. Create teacher survey form b. Survey teachers c. Compile results of teachers' assessments d. Compile results of standardized tests	a. Feb 15–25 (Year 1) b. Mar 1–Mar 15 c. Mar 15–30 d. April 1–15	a. Evaluation coordinator b. Evaluation coordinator c. Evaluation coordinator; interns; science eval committee d. Evaluation coordinator	Duplication of forms and reports: $50 Postage for disseminating final report: $25

Evaluation Questions	Tasks	Task Beginning and End Date	Personnel Involved	Other Resources Needed and Costs
	e. Review of overall findings	e. April 15–May 15	e. Evaluation coordinator; interns, science eval committee	
	f. Share with science teachers for feedback	f. May 15	f. Evaluation coordinator	
	g. Revise report	g. May 15–June 1	g. Evaluation coordinator	
	h. Incorporate findings from Steps 1–3 into comprehensive final report	h. June 1–June 30	h. Evaluation coordinator; interns, science evaluation committee	Duplication and printing Costs: $50; Postage for disseminating final report: $25
SCHOOL YEAR 2 5. To what extent is the curriculum meeting our expectations?	a. Review curriculum standards from multiple sources; compare to current	a. Sept 1–15 (Year 2)	a-d. Evaluation coordinator; science evaluation committee; interns	
	b. Compare areas targeted by curriculum to strengths and weaknesses in student outcomes	b. Sept 15–Oct 15		
	c. Analyze science curriculum to see what is feasible, given limitations in time and resources	c. Oct 15–Oct 30		
	d. Summarize strengths and weaknesses	d. Nov 1–30		
	e. Share synopses with science teachers, principal	e. Dec 1	e-f. Evaluation coordinator	
	f. Incorporate feedback into final report	f-g. Dec 1–20		
	g. Make recommendations for revising curricula and instruction and for purchasing resources		g. Evaluation coordinator; science evaluation committee	

4

Organizing and Analyzing Information

For each evaluation question on the worksheet, you will now want to describe the way in which the information will be analyzed. This is important, because you can often be swamped with information. How can you summarize the information you collect so that the message from your data is accurate and clear? Several techniques will be considered in this section for analyzing qualitative (narrative) and quantitative (numerical) information and the means for conducting the analysis, such as using statistical software on a computer, using a panel of readers from the staff of your school, or even hiring a consultant. If the consultant route is taken, it is best to involve the consultant in the very beginning of the evaluation planning. Do not wait until the information has been collected to seek outside help in analyzing it. The United States is full of overstocked data warehouses where unanalyzed information sits unused because of short-sightedness in the planning for data analysis. A little planning can save a lot of work at this point.

ORGANIZING AND ANALYZING QUALITATIVE INFORMATION

The best advice for organizing narrative information (e.g., field notes, transcripts of interviews, written responses to open-ended questions, and copies of documents) includes the following:

1. Make sure it is all there.

2. Make copies for safe storage, for writing on, and for cutting and pasting.

3. Organize it as it comes in. Three hours of work organizing and summarizing for each hour of work collecting is a good rule of thumb. Some ways of filing information are by topic (e.g., school climate, teaching methods), by respondents (e.g., teacher data, student data), by event (e.g., the science fair), or by calendar (e.g., September data). For example, all information about the effectiveness of a new teaching unit can be filed together. There are numerous computer software packages for advanced analyses of qualitative data.[1] However, for simple analyses, basic word processing programs or spreadsheets such as Excel may suffice.

4. Take stock during data collection and at the end about what you are finding.

5. Use your human computer (your brain) to draw conclusions and then back them up with the information you have collected. That is, make the best case you can for your findings.

6. Verify and validate your findings by getting reactions from people who were there.

The best analyses of qualitative data use intellectual rigor and documentation to support conclusions.

Resources on qualitative analysis include Huberman & Miles (2002) and M. Q. Patton (2001).

ORGANIZING AND ANALYZING QUANTITATIVE INFORMATION

Sometimes program evaluation information will be numerical data that will require some form of statistical analysis to create a meaningful and accurate summary. Consider the methods and instruments listed in Chapter 3 and the kinds of data each will generate. You can plan your quantitative data analyses by considering each method or instrument and how you will deal with the data it generates.

Testing

Norm-referenced standardized testing companies typically will provide a clear, easily interpreted summary for your school, for each classroom, and for individual students if requested. In program evaluation, one usually is most interested in classroom and school statistics. The use of each of the following types of statistics is illustrated in the following pages in the context of data that may be collected in a program evaluation.

The *mean,* or average raw score, tells us how a typical student in the classroom or building performed. Because the mean will correspond to a fictional student, the score does not reflect the performance of any one individual. It does represent the performance level of the class or the school in the form of an "individual."

A frequency distribution tells us how many students scored at each score level in the classroom or the school. This gives us better information about how the class is doing than does the mean alone. Bar charts or other graphs can be used to report this information.

The *variance* or *standard deviation* tells us how spread out the students' scores are for a given classroom or school. The more spread out or heterogeneous the group is, the bigger the value of the variance or standard deviation will be. By comparing standard deviations across classrooms or schools, or by comparing them to standard deviations of zero, you can see how close together or spread apart the students in any one classroom, grade level, or school actually are. For example, if the standard deviation of this year's 10th-grade standardized achievement test raw scores in science is 4.80 and last year it was 12.50 for the 10th grade, we could conclude that this year the 10th graders were performing much more alike than 10th graders did last year. They are more homogeneous in science achievement this year.

Survey Questionnaire or Interview

You usually will be most interested in the responses to each question on the questionnaire. Consequently, you should list each question and then summarize the responses for the question. For structured questions where respondents check one option out of several provided, you would do as follows:

1. (List the questions)	(frequency)	(percentage)
a. (list answer options)		
b.		
c.		
d.		

An example of reporting summary statistics for structured questionnaire items is shown below.

Do you plan to be involved in future science inservice activities?		
Yes	78	54.9%
Not sure	19	13.4%
No (retired)	1	0.7%
No response	44	31.0%

As indicated above, you should provide the frequency (tally) and percentage response for each option. The frequency distribution in this example shows that a majority (54.9%) of respondents plan to be involved in future science inservice activities. For some reason, there was a large number of people who did not respond to the question. One might want to contact those 44 people again to ask them why they did not respond.

For open-ended questions where respondents write a short response, you would again list the question and then provide the verbatim responses if there is a small number of respondents (e.g., less than 20). Then, give a verbal summary of the responses. If there is a large number of respondents, categories of responses should be formed, and then the frequencies and percentages of responses falling into each category should be reported.

Sometimes you will be interested in seeing if there is a relationship between responses on one item and responses on another item on the survey form. An example of this is shown below.

How many years have you been teaching?	Do you plan to attend future science inservice activities?	
	Yes	No/Not Sure
0–5	48	0
6–10	20	0
11–15	9	10
Over 15	1	10

You may use *a correlation coefficient* to describe a relationship when responses are numbers (e.g., age, test score, or amount of time on task). It is obvious just from looking at this example that the younger teachers are most likely to attend future science inservice activities. This helps program coordinators target their presentations.

Attitude Scales

The formats for attitude scales differ across instruments, and it is hard to make general statements about the best approach to data analysis. One of the most common formats, however, is a Likert scale in which a statement is given and the respondent is to respond on a 5-point scale labeled "strongly agree" on one end and "strongly disagree" on the other. In this case, each item can be analyzed as follows:

	Strongly Agree	Agree	Not Sure	Disagree	Strongly Disagree
1. *(Statement)*	frequency percentage				

mean score =
standard deviation =

The frequency and percentage of responses at each scale point can be recorded, and then the mean and standard deviation for the responses can be calculated. This would be done for each item. An example follows:

	Strongly Agree	Agree	Not Sure	Disagree	Strongly Disagree
1. The new science textbook teaches students how to solve problems on their own.	139 19.6%	396 55.9%	107 15.1%	56 7.9%	11 1.6%

mean score = 3.84
standard deviation = 2.15

In this example, about 75% of the teachers agreed or strongly agreed that the new science textbook teaches problem solving. The mean, or average, is close to the "agree" point on the scale (3.84). The standard deviation (2.15) tells us there was not perfect agreement, that is, there was some spread in the responses.

If the Likert scale has been developed so that all statements are getting at the same issue in different ways, a total score can be calculated for each respondent, and then the total scores can be analyzed for a group of respondents as though they were test scores. In other words, a mean, standard deviation, and frequency distribution can be calculated to summarize the total group of scores.

Analyzing Quantitative Checklist Information

Again, observation checklists vary greatly in format, and it is hard to provide a general procedure for data analysis that would hold for all cases. In many cases, frequency counts will suffice. Usually, however, the guide that accompanies a published observation checklist will provide procedures for data analysis. In most cases, procedures that have already been discussed will be used to summarize observations—means, standard deviations, and frequency distributions—to describe group data. Correlation coefficients may be used to relate one observed behavior to another.

These are the techniques used most often in quantitative data analysis. For further information and computational procedures, see the following sources: Gonick & Smith (1993), Hopkins, Hopkins, & Glass (1996), and Jaeger (1990).

INTERPRETING THE INFORMATION

Once the information for the evaluation has been collected and analyzed, the job of evaluation is not done. In fact, in one sense it is just beginning, because the process of evaluation involves both description and judgment. The final step before reporting the results is to attach value judgments to the information now available. What does it mean for your program? What are the implications for program improvement? For change? These are questions that the evaluators should not answer alone; the major stakeholders should respond as well.

Numbers do not speak for themselves. Each member of your group will have a concept of what the data mean. This is to be expected because of different experiences, training, roles in the program, expectations, and educational philosophies. Your group's members simply are not all the same person and would not all come up with the same set of recommendations after reviewing the information collected in the program evaluation.

Consequently, it is advised that you organize a stakeholder meeting. About two weeks before the meeting, information summaries should be sent to each meeting participant. The information should be organized by evaluation question so that all of the information pertaining to each question is displayed under that question. Participants should then be asked to read and digest all of this information about the program and to come to the meeting prepared to answer the following questions:

1. *What are the strengths and what are the weaknesses of this program?* Be able to support your statements with data.

2. *What are the implications of your analysis for changing the program?* That is, what are the areas that need improvement?

Reporting Realities: Inaccuracies Created by Improper Evaluation Management and Reporting

The superintendent of a large urban district hired an evaluator to assess the school climate at each school. The evaluator developed a 75-item survey based on input from the superintendent and school board. It was pilot-tested on a small group of subjects and found to be adequately reliable and valid.

The evaluator mailed a packet of surveys to the principal of each school. The principal was to distribute the surveys to all the school staff, then collect them after they were completed. The packet contained a cover letter that described the evaluation, the processes of administering and collecting the surveys, and the date that the evaluator would arrive to visit the school and collect all the completed surveys. The evaluator called the principals a few days after the packets of surveys were mailed to make sure they had arrived and had been distributed.

A month later, the evaluator visited each school to pick up the packet of completed surveys as well as conduct some interviews. She had not bothered to remind the principals to make sure the surveys were completed and turned in. At some schools, all or most of the surveys had been completed and returned as promised. At others, the embarrassed principals apologized for only receiving a few completed surveys. The evaluator had extra surveys on hand, which the principals hastily distributed to their staff and implored them to complete before the evaluator left at the end of the day. At two schools, the principals threatened to sanction the teachers if the surveys were not completed and returned to them that same day.

The evaluator did not record these circumstances surrounding the survey administration. The staff who entered the data noticed that at some of the schools, a lot of the surveys had large amounts of missing or self-contradicting data. This was especially problematic at two of the schools, where the items that were completed yielded particularly low scores concerning opinions of the principals. However, since the data entry staff had only been asked to enter the data, they did not mention these phenomena to the evaluator. The evaluator noticed the missing data but decided that it was too cumbersome to report the response rate for each item at each school. Besides, the response rates were impressively high. She decided to report the means and standard deviations of the various scores for each site, letting the numbers speak for themselves. She did not share the results with any representatives of the respective schools for further interpretation before finalizing the report.

Stakeholder Meetings

At the meeting, each participant, including the evaluators, should be allowed to speak without interruption. A summary of the comments provided at the meeting should be part of the evaluation report. Where there are areas of common agreement, this fact should be noted. Where there are minority views, these too should be noted. This interpretation process will provide direction for program development in the coming years. It will also provide an important role in the evaluation for key stakeholders. Because of this, it is a critical step in the evaluation process.

Beyond the stakeholder meeting, you also have a responsibility to report how the program compares to known standards:

- Program goals
- Standards set by national organizations
- Standards set by model school districts or models based on professional literature (e.g., "what works"[2] or "effective schools")

This chapter can be summarized by the following key points:

1. Select a method for analyzing qualitative and quantitative information that is appropriate for each evaluation question and the method used to collect the information.

2. Involve key stakeholders in interpreting the meaning and implications of the evaluation results.

ILLUSTRATIVE CASE STUDY (PART 5)

Mr. Henry further developed the earlier evaluation plan (see Table 3.2) by adding a column that delineated who would be responsible for analyzing the various forms of data they collected (see Table 4.1). He wanted to make sure a wide range of stakeholders was involved.

By December, all the data regarding the teacher's outcomes, topics for the fall semester, and time on each topic had been analyzed by the interns (see row 2 in Table 4.1). They quantified the time spent on each topic and compared it to the time recommended by experts in the field. They interpreted the results of particular data with help from a literature review.[3] Eventually they came up with the following preliminary results and interpretations, which they e-mailed to all of the science teachers two weeks prior to a staff meeting dedicated to discussing them:

- Both the outcomes and lesson plans included numerous topics beyond the expectations of the curriculum.
- The new, state-mandated topics of the curriculum were often missing, incomplete, or appeared slapped on without being incorporated into the rest of the topics and lesson plans.
- Insufficient time appeared to be devoted to areas that were new to the curriculum. They seemed to be squeezed between old lessons rather than being integrated within them.

Some of the teachers were concerned that these findings could be used against them. Mr. Henry reassured them that all the data was confidential and no one was identified by name. In fact, this portion of the report would not be released to the school board, because it could not be fully interpreted without the rest of the evaluation's data, which had yet to be collected. However, the teachers could contact Mr. Henry if they wanted to know how they fared as individuals.

A couple of teachers complained that the findings occurred because they were expected to cover more areas without adequate instructional guides or up-to-date materials. "That's a part of our evaluation we will cover down the road," Mr. Henry explained. "One of our four main evaluation questions is, Do we have the resources we need to cover the areas required by the curriculum? The answers to this question will help us further interpret the findings we have so far."

"Of course some of these teachers won't have the time or resources for the stuff they're *supposed* to teach," opined one teacher. "Let's face it. They're spending all their time pushing their personal agendas on what they think kids should know." This led to impassioned arguments that most of the original topics, outcome goals, and lesson plans were at least as appropriate as those of the revised curriculum; some were adamant that they shouldn't compromise them because of some new federal mandate that was out of touch with the needs of their students.

Mr. Henry cut in just as the air became uncomfortably tense. "The NCLB mandates and consequences are here to stay, whether we like them or not," he explained. "The question is, instead of complaining about them, can we work to improve the test scores without sacrificing our school-level objectives?"

"But how well are we doing on our school-level objectives?" asked Ms. Garcia.

"That's the next step in the evaluation. The results of that won't be out until June."

Table 4.1 Evaluation Information Collection and Analysis Worksheet (All Columns Completed)

Evaluation Questions	Why the Question Is Important	Information Needed to Answer the Question	When and How the Information Will Be Collected	Analysis and Interpretation
1. Are the expected student outcomes of the science classes congruent with the school's overall science curriculum?	1. We need to have goals that are in line with the curriculum.	1. What each teacher of science expects; what our curriculum guides say	1. In September, each teacher of science will be asked to list the 10 most important outcomes for students in science this year.	1. A grade-by-grade listing of what teachers provided will be compared to curriculum guides and will be evaluated by the science committee.
2. What topics are covered by grade level, and is sufficient time spent on each?	2. We need to know what we are doing to meet our goals.	2. What each teacher covers; what our curriculum guides say	2. In September, each science teacher will be asked to provide his or her lesson plan outline for the year.	2. A grade-by-grade listing of topics and times spent on each will be analyzed by the graduate interns. A preliminary report will then be shared with the teachers for feedback and revisions.
3. What methods and materials are used for each topic, and how good are they?	3. We need to analyze our instruction to identify targets for improvement.	3. What each teacher uses; teachers' judgments of strengths and weaknesses of methods and materials	3. In January, each science teacher will be asked to list methods and materials for each topic and to evaluate each.	3. A list of methods and materials will be prepared in February. This will be evaluated by the science evaluation committee.

(Continued)

53

Table 4.1 (Continued)

Evaluation Questions	Why the Question Is Important	Information Needed to Answer the Question	When and How the Information Will Be Collected	Analysis and Interpretation
4. How well are students performing on the expected outcomes?	4. We need to know how well we are meeting our goals	4. Achievement of students in science according to a wide variety of teacher-selected and standardized assessments	4. In February, each science teacher will be asked to list strong and weak outcomes of their students. In April, standardized state assessment science scores will be compiled.	4. A grade-by-grade listing of strengths and weaknesses of students in science will be prepared in June by the science evaluation committee.
5. To what extent is the curriculum meeting our expectations?	5. We need to be clear about our standards and the extent to which we are meeting them.	5. The data from the above four questions	5. Starting the following September, staff will compare the strengths and weaknesses in the outcomes and the limitations of the materials to the expectations of the current curriculum.	5. The curriculum will be assessed, and recommendations to change it will be made on the basis of which areas need the most improvement and what resources are available or can feasibly be obtained.

This brings us to Chapter 5, which will discuss the reporting of information

NOTES

1. For information on software to analyze qualitative data, please see www .eval.org/EvaluationLinks/QDA.htm.

2. The "what works clearinghouse" criteria for adequate research is somewhat controversial in the field of evaluation and research. See http://www.eval .org/doepage.htm for more on this topic.

3. For an example related to this portion of the case, see Newmann, Smith, Allensworth, & Bryk (2001).

5

Reporting Information

Throughout the course of the evaluation, it is wise to keep participants and stakeholders informed about the evaluation process and the progress being made toward its completion. When preparing the final report of the evaluation, you need to keep in mind the purpose of the evaluation, the major audiences (decision makers) for the results, and the best medium to communicate with each audience.

AUDIENCES

The evaluation will often have other teachers as the main audience. To overlook any of them would be a mistake. Typically, you will also want to share your recommendations with others, such as a member of the school board, the superintendent, your building principal, a parent group, or other participants in the evaluation. It will be important to consider what questions each wanted to have addressed and then to consider the best way to communicate with each audience. In some school studies, modest forms of reporting evaluation findings and recommendations, such as a memo, committee report, or program plan, may be most appropriate. Uploading reports to a school or district Web site is an effective form of communication to larger audiences.

REVIEW OF DRAFT REPORT

Once a draft report is completed, you should circulate the draft to key stakeholders for comments. This is an important step, because even the smallest factual errors can be used to discredit the evaluation. Evaluators are human, and it cannot be assumed that the report will be completely accurate and omniscient. Reviewers could be asked to comment on the following:

- Factual errors
- Typing errors
- Plausible interpretations that are missing
- Additional evidence that might have been missed
- Any other suggestions that might improve the writing style or appearance of the report

Once comments are received, the report can be revised using your best judgments about what to use and what to ignore.

Short reports are most likely to be read. Teachers may be most interested in things that pertain to them or their role in the program. A one-page summary hitting the high points of the evaluation—what was evaluated, the purpose of the evaluation, major findings (strengths and weaknesses), and recommendations—may best fit the needs of many stakeholders. If the evaluation uncovered controversial or questionable issues that targeted specific stakeholders, sharing these findings one-on-one with the concerned stakeholders before sending the draft to a wider audience may prevent defensive reactions (see Shooting the Messenger).

A useful guide to communicating evaluation results is Torres, Preskill, & Piontek (2005).

Shooting the Messenger, or Messenger Shooting Himself in the Foot?

An external evaluator from a small firm was hired to evaluate a new districtwide elementary school literacy program. He looked at context, structure, processes, and outcomes of the program at each school. He chose interviews with the staff as well as teacher surveys, student surveys, and students' test results as the methods.

The results were fairly positive at all of the schools except for one. At this school not only were there no improvements in students' reading and writing test scores, but there were numerous complaints from the teachers about how the principal had made it difficult to implement the new curriculum: vague, shifting expectations about what the program's goals were; insufficient time to prepare the lessons; and attempts to implement numerous other changes throughout the school at the same time. The report included several candid quotes from teachers expressing their disgust with the principal's leadership.

As promised in the original contract, the evaluator turned in a final report to the school superintendent at the end of the evaluation. He also, as originally planned, presented the results to the district board during a meeting and published the results on the district's Web site.

Several days after the report was published, the evaluator and his supervisor received an irate letter from the principal of the school that had received the poor review. She explained that the evaluator had never told her that she herself would be evaluated as a principal or that her school would be compared to others. She also pointed out numerous (rather trivial) errors in the report, as she repeatedly questioned the evaluator's competence.

As the evaluator discussed the letter with his frustrated supervisor, he vacillated between feeling guilty for offending the principal and furious for being attacked without justification.

"But I *did* tell the principal that we would be looking at structure and implementation issues," he explained to his supervisor.

The supervisor asked, "But did you report these sensitive findings directly to the principal before you shared them with the superintendent, the school board, and the general public?"

"No," he replied. "I just stuck with the original, agreed-upon plan for dissemination."

The supervisor sighed. "In the future, if you come up with results that are this incendiary, it's best to personally notify the individual who is most directly affected, deliver a draft for her to review, and discuss it with her one-on-one. If you had done so in this case, the principal would have given her perspective on what was going on, beyond your original interview with her. It probably wouldn't have changed your overall report much. Still, the principal might have even used the findings constructively rather than reacted to them defensively."

USING THE RESULTS OF A PROGRAM EVALUATION

One of the fundamental principles of program evaluation is that the evaluation should not be done if it is not going to be used. It is a waste of scarce resources to invest time in an evaluation that sits on a shelf or receives no follow-up. So, assuming that the program evaluation will be used, you need to consider how it will be used and how you can facilitate its use. As noted in Chapter 1, the evaluators should consider the many payoffs of program evaluation. How could the program evaluation be used to improve the school program?

First, target the program evaluation report to the use(s) where it will do the most good for the school building. Then, make a commitment to help other program staff use the evaluation results. Finally, assist other staff in reviewing the results and translating them into a plan of action that will then be implemented. A follow-up evaluation may then determine whether the actions taken have strengthened the program. The plan of action for the program might include plans to keep the district administration and the public informed and may also be used as a basis for planning staff development for the program staff. For more information about creating useful evaluations, please see Patton (1997).

This chapter can be summarized by the following key points:

1. Identify the audiences that should receive information about the program.

2. Choose an appropriate method and time to report findings to each audience.

3. Follow up to see that the evaluation findings are translated into an appropriate plan of action.

ILLUSTRATIVE CASE STUDY (PART 6)

Mr. Henry's previous meeting with the anxious science teachers emphasized the importance of clarifying who would receive reports of which information in which forms. He anticipated some real interest in the findings of the completed Year 1 science evaluation, not only from teachers but also from parents and the school board. They knew about the evaluation and naturally would be curious about the results.

Mr. Henry called a meeting of the science evaluation committee to discuss who should receive what information using what means of communication. The other teachers at Lakeview Elementary School and Ms. Goss were obvious audiences, but the committee decided to prepare a report to parents and to the school board as well. Ms. Radisson then frowned reflectively and said, "You know, the superintendent will need to approve anything we send to parents or the school board. We'd better include her as an audience too."

"Good idea," agreed Mr. Henry.

"The middle school principals might want to share our recommendations with their science teachers too," said Mr. Williams. "And come to think of it, I'll bet the other elementary schools would be interested in what we're planning. We should include the elementary principals as an audience."

"Right on. Now, should we use the same report for all audiences?" asked Mr. Henry.

After some discussion, the committee decided to use a question-and-answer format for Ms. Goss and the other teachers at Lakeview Elementary School. Each evaluation question would be followed by tables, qualitative findings, interpretations, and recommendations. The purposes, procedures, and recommendations would be written as a brief executive summary for interested parents, the school board, and personnel in the other buildings. Availability of the summary would be announced to parents through the school district newsletter, and on the school Web site. If any of these audiences wanted more detailed information, they would be sent a copy of the results reported to Ms. Goss and the Lakeview Elementary School teachers.

The members also agreed that a time schedule for implementing the recommendations would be part of the report going to Ms. Goss and the Lakeview teachers. Before any report went out, however, they further agreed that a draft would be reviewed by Ms. Goss and anyone she would want to involve. They wanted to make sure that the reports were accurate and clear. They were also open to suggestions for improving the recommendations and the implementation plan.

Chapter 6, the final chapter of this guide, provides information on the administration of a program evaluation.

6

Administering the Evaluation

A program evaluation can be fairly complex. The logistics can be overwhelming at times, time schedules can place a burden on all who are involved, budgets need to be watched, and colleagues will need supervision and guidance. Then there are the politics of the school, interpersonal relationships to nurture, the communication needs of participants, ethical considerations, and, of course, the unforeseen. Dealing with all of this takes a well-organized person or group and a good management plan. It also takes some flexibility, tolerance for ambiguity, and a sense of humor. This is no small order.

DEVELOPING A MANAGEMENT PLAN FOR THE EVALUATION

In Chapter 3, details of a science program evaluation were worked out on a set of sample worksheets (Figure 2.2). From the second set of worksheets (Tables 3.2, 3.4, and 4.1), you can develop a list of assignments and a budget.

To establish assignments, first make a list of the different people whose names appear on the worksheets, then indicate across calendar months how much of each person's time will be required. Using information from Table 3.2, personnel needs (number of hours for each month) could be summarized as shown in Table 6.1.

For complex projects, project management software such as Microsoft Project can save considerable time and effort. However, for relatively simple projects such as the one in our case, basic spreadsheet or word processing programs such as Excel, WordPerfect, or Microsoft Word may suffice.

Table 6.1 Sample Management Plan for the Evaluation (Year 1)

| | Month | | | | | | | | | |
Personnel	Sept	Oct	Nov	Dec	Jan	Feb	Mar	Apr	May	June
Evaluation coordinator	10	10	30	10	10	8	2	1	20	20
Graduate interns (each)	10	10	20	20		10	10	5	20	20
Science evaluation committee members (each)	2		5	5		5	5		5	10

Note: Time allotments are listed in hours.

Budget

The budget is also based on the worksheets for the illustrative case study:

	Year One	Year Two
Duplication	$140	$50
Postage	$25	$75
Materials	$25	
Total	$190	$125

These figures are the totals of those found in Table 3.4. As you can see, this evaluation was possible to conduct on a shoestring budget. Because school staff are already being paid for their time, personnel time does not reflect new costs to the school district. Rather, these are already-paid-for resources that are being reassigned to do the evaluation. Furthermore, the interns did not need to be paid for their time, as it was part of their graduate school program. Simple e-mail technology saves considerable resources, reducing the needs for printed copies and postage.

Time Schedules

Finally, a time schedule needs to be developed, again based on the illustrative case study worksheets. There are two types of time charts commonly used in program evaluation. The first is called a *Gantt chart*; it is used to plot evaluation activities (tasks) across the time period planned for the project. This type of chart helps to visualize when peak busy times will occur. The Gantt chart developed by Mr. Henry in the illustrative case study is shown in Figure 6.1.

A second type of time chart is called an *activity network.* It plots activities and milestones along the way to the end product. This chart helps to visualize those activities that can go on simultaneously and those that are dependent on earlier activities. Like the Gantt chart, it can also be used to monitor progress on the evaluation to ensure that things are getting done

Figure 6.1 Gantt Chart for Program Evaluation (Year 1)

Evaluation Question	Activity	Sep	Oct	Nov	Dec	Jan	Feb	Mar	Apr	May	Jun
1.	a. Create teacher survey forms	//									
	b. Survey teachers	//									
	c. Compile results		//								
	d. Compare to curriculum		//								
	e. Prepare report of strengths and weaknesses			//							
2.	a. Lit review on best practices in instruction	////									
	b. Collect outlines of lesson plans from teachers	//									
	c. Compare lesson plans to best practices and to curriculum		////								
	d. Prepare preliminary report of strengths and weaknesses			//							
	e. Share with science teachers for feedback			//							
	f. Revise report				///						
3.	a. Create teacher survey form					//					
	b. Survey teachers					//					
	c. Compile results						//				
	d. Review of findings						//				
	e. Prepare report of strengths and weaknesses							////			
4.	a. Create teacher survey form						//				
	b. Survey teachers							//			
	c. Compile results of teachers' assessments							//			
	d. Compile results of standardized tests								//		
	e. Review of overall findings									////	
	f. Share with science teachers for feedback									/	
	g. Revise report									//	
	h. Incorporate findings from Steps 1–3 into comprehensive final report										////

Figure 6.2 Activity Network for Program Evaluation

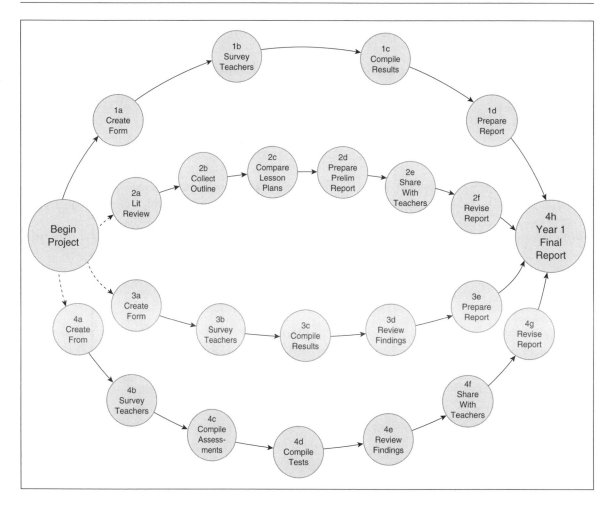

on time. The activity network developed by Mr. Henry (using the example of Table 3.2) is presented in Figure 6.2.

These management tools will help the evaluation coordinator keep on schedule and within budget. Alone, however, they will not guarantee a successful project. Careful monitoring of the quality of work, cooperation by staff, need for revising the project plan, and need to adapt to unforeseen events should also occupy your mind.

Politics, Ethics, and the Interpersonal Aspects of Program Evaluation

Evaluation is a human activity, and it is accompanied by interesting forms of human behavior. The politics of evaluation produce undue pressure on the evaluator or participants in the evaluation. Forms of this pressure are lack of cooperation, attempts to derail the evaluation, attempts to discredit it, or attempts to influence its outcome(s). It is hard to foresee when, if ever, political influences may appear, but there are some things that evaluators can do to minimize their role.

Dealing With School Politics

1. Establish and maintain open communications among evaluators and stakeholders.

2. Anticipate political pressures and try to meet them head on through private meetings or, if that does not work, assistance from a supervisor.

3. Involve in the evaluation all individuals or groups who may have a vested interest in its outcomes.

4. Have frequent meetings and informal chats to keep people informed about the evaluation and to enlist their support.

5. Write the report carefully and submit a draft for review comments to key stakeholders.

Ethical Considerations

The ethics of evaluation are a concern when one considers the way in which participants are treated. If confidential records or other information is collected, the evaluators are bound to protect that confidentiality, usually by keeping data under lock and key. Participants need to be protected from embarrassment or harassment. Individuals should not be identified in reports unless they give permission. They should be treated with diplomacy and respect; they should not be subjected to any form of physical or psychological harm or even potential for harm. If data are being collected from students, most school districts have policies about parental permission. You need to remain aboveboard and neutral in the collection of information and the making of recommendations. You must honor promises and commitments. You must also be incorruptible, reporting any possible conflicts of interest or attempts to influence the outcomes of the evaluation. This is a tall order, but given the stake that many people have in the results of a program evaluation, trust and credibility are essential ingredients to a successful evaluation.

A useful reference in this case is Newman & Brown (1996).

Interpersonal Relations

Interpersonal relationships can be strained if the evaluator is demanding, undiplomatic, or insensitive to the feelings of others. Protocol violations will also lead to interpersonal strain. You should make every effort to understand the views of participants and to honor them. Evaluators should be good listeners, especially about the evaluation, and maintain good communications about the evaluation with participants. Evaluators should also avoid disruption of routines and work schedules to the greatest extent possible.

This chapter can be summarized by the following key points:

1. Develop a management plan for the evaluation that details assignments, a budget, and a time schedule.

2. Attend to the political, ethical, and interpersonal dimensions of the evaluation from beginning to end.

ILLUSTRATIVE CASE STUDY (PART 7)

With most of the details of the evaluation study worked out, Mr. Henry has pulled them together into an effective management plan. As he reflects on the careful planning that has gone into the evaluation of Lakeview Elementary School's science program, he cannot help but feel secure about the rest of the study. Having a detailed road map makes the job much easier and allows him to be comfortable with the fact that he now really does know what he is doing. He is especially pleased to learn that both the PTA and the discipline committee are in the process of planning their own evaluations and are seeking his assistance in organizing and managing them.

Mr. Henry can now attend to what many consider the small things in program evaluation: the items that he knows can become big things if left unattended. Fortunately, he is in a school where most people work well together. Historically, the school has had some resistance to change. However, this has abated as staff have been reassured that subsequent changes will be based on thorough evaluation, which includes everyone's input. Occasionally the pressure from—and the controversy concerning—NCLB mandates have caused tension and conflict. Mr. Henry attempts to minimize these by redirecting teachers to the common goal of a well-rounded education in science, which includes, but is not limited to, NCLB requirements. He will keep his sensors out and attempt to address any potential problems before they become real.

"This evaluation business isn't so bad after all," he thinks as he walks down the hallway. He is pleased that Lakeview Elementary will now have an official School Improvement Plan that is more than a stack of paperwork used to fulfill an outside mandate. The evaluation will be used to genuinely improve numerous aspects of the school's science program and may have consequences for Lakeview City's youth for years to come.

Epilogue

This guide started with the statement that there are two things one should remember about evaluating programs in education. First, not everyone will see the program in the same light, and this pluralism should be reflected in the program evaluation report. Second, attend to three characteristics of good program evaluation—communication, communication, and communication. Having completed the six chapters of this guide, you should have a better understanding of and appreciation for the basis of these statements. It is now time to put these guidelines into practice.

OTHER RESOURCES

There are numerous other references for further information about conducting quality evaluations. Resource A is an annotated bibliography of recommended textbooks regarding evaluation in general. Resource B lists various Web sites pertinent to evaluators. As an aid to evaluating student performance, Resource C lists an outline of Bloom's classic taxonomy of cognitive objectives.

The Joint Committee on Standards for Educational Evaluation, a coalition of 16 professional organizations concerned with the quality of evaluations in education, has published program evaluation standards. These standards may be used to assess the quality of any program evaluation. A summary of the standards appears in Resource D.

Resource A

Annotated Bibliography on Program Evaluation

Fitzpatrick, J. L., Sanders, J. R., & Worthen, B. R. (2004). *Program evaluation* (3rd ed.). Boston: Allyn & Bacon.

This text is divided into five sections. The first covers the theoretical, historical, and philosophical foundations of program evaluation. The second provides descriptions of alternative approaches to program evaluation. The third and fourth provide practical guidelines for planning, conducting, and using program evaluations. The practical guidelines cover clarifying the evaluation request and responsibilities; setting boundaries and analyzing the evaluation context; identifying and selecting the evaluative questions, criteria, and issues; planning information collection, analysis, and interpretation; developing a management plan; dealing with political, ethical, and interpersonal aspects of evaluation; reporting and using evaluation information; and evaluating evaluations. The fifth addresses emerging and future settings for program evaluation. A case study example runs through the practical guidelines sections.

Herman, J. L. (Ed.). (1987). *Program evaluation kit* (2nd ed.). Newbury Park, CA: Sage.

This classic collection is a practical guide to the entire evaluation process, from evaluation design to reporting. The kit includes handy tips, exercises, data collection forms, flowcharts, graphs, measurement instruments, and other illustrative items. The nine volumes in the kit are as follows: *Evaluator's Handbook* (Vol. 1), *How to Focus an Evaluation* (Vol. 2), *How to Design a Program Evaluation* (Vol. 3), *How to Use Qualitative Methods in Evaluation* (Vol. 4), *How to Assess Program Implementation* (Vol. 5), *How to Measure Attitudes* (Vol. 6), *How to Measure Performance and Use Tests* (Vol. 7), *How to Analyze Data* (Vol. 8), and *How to Communicate Evaluation Findings* (Vol. 9).

Hopkins, K. D. (1998). *Educational and psychological measurement and evaluation* (8th ed.). Boston: Allyn & Bacon.

One of the best available references for constructing achievement tests, this textbook also provides readable explanations of the concepts of measurement validity and reliability. Chapters on standardized aptitude, achievement, interest, and social measures provide a useful overview of available standardized instruments.

Jaeger, R. M. (1990). *Statistics: A spectator sport* (2nd ed.). Newbury Park, CA: Sage.
This book is for those who want to develop an understanding of the use and interpretation of statistics commonly used in education. It contains clear explanations and many practical examples in the areas of measures of central tendency and variability, correlation, and hypothesis testing when comparing group averages.

Joint Committee on Standards for Educational Evaluation. (1994). *The program evaluation standards.* Thousand Oaks, CA: Sage.
How do you know if a program evaluation has been planned or done well? Apply the Joint Committee's standards to the design or final report. This listing of 30 standards for program evaluation is the authoritative reference on principles of good program evaluation. Sponsored by 16 professional associations concerned with the quality of program evaluations in education, the Joint Committee has defined state-of-the-art principles, guidelines, and illustrative cases that can be used to judge the quality of any program evaluation. The standards fall into four categories with regard to the evaluation: utility, feasibility, propriety, and accuracy (see Resource D).

Patton, M. Q. (1997). *Utilization-focused evaluation: The new century text* (3rd ed.) Thousand Oaks, CA: Sage.
Using humorous yet enlightening stories and illustrations, this book provides an overview of a wide range of evaluation methods. The unifying theme of the book is how to select and implement evaluation methods that will yield evaluations that will be useful to their stakeholders.

Stufflebeam, D. L. (2001). *Evaluation models: New directions for evaluation, No. 89.* San Francisco: Jossey-Bass.
This monograph thoroughly describes 22 evaluation approaches and compares and contrasts their various strengths and weaknesses. The approaches are categorized as Questions/Methods, Improvement/Accountability, and Social Agenda/Advocacy. A fourth category of illegitimate "Pseudoevaluations" is also described. Numerous checklists are included to aid readers in selecting a legitimate model that is most appropriate to their particular evaluation needs.

United Way of America. (1996). *Measuring program outcomes.* Alexandria, VA: Author.
This guide provides a very practical step-by-step overview of the process of developing logic models and then using them to design outcome measures as part of the program evaluation process. This guide is used throughout the United States for training evaluators in outcomes measurement.

Resource B

Evaluation-Related Web Sites

http://www.eval.org

    The American Evaluation Association describes activities, conferences, programs of the organization, lists local affiliates and topical interest groups, presents *The Guiding Principles of Evaluation* as well as the Joint Committee standards, and provides links to collections of evaluation resources, foundations that fund evaluation activities, and governmental organizations and NGOs that conduct evaluation activities. It also provides links to numerous other evaluation associations within the United States and in other countries.

http://www.bama.ua.edu/archives/evaltalk.html

    This site gives instructions on how to register for participation in EvalTalk, the American Evaluation Association Listserv, which conducts an active online discussion of evaluation issues. For other questions about EvalTalk, contact the listowners, Kathy Bolland at kbolland@sw.ua.edu or Carolyn Sullins at carolyn.sullins@wmich.edu.

http://www.wmich.edu/evalctr

    The Evaluation Center at Western Michigan University contains checklists, papers, reports, glossary of evaluation terms, bibliographies, information on the Joint Committee and the standards it developed for program evaluation, personnel and student evaluation, and a directory of evaluators.

http://www.unl.edu/buros

    The Oscar and Luella Buros Center for Testing provides resources for assessment, consultation, and outreach. It gives advice on test development, evaluation, and oversight. This organization conducts audit, accreditation, research, and consultation services for organizations wanting to improve their evaluation and testing practices.

http://www.cse.ucla.edu

    The site for Center for Research on Evaluation, Standards, and Student Testing includes reports, policy briefs, newsletters, a test locator, and school portfolios.

http://www.ets.org

    The Web site for the Educational Testing Service, this site provides information on assessment in higher education.

http://www.eval.org/hstlinks.htm

This Web site contains the American Evaluation Association's statements on high-stakes testing currently used in 49 states. It also includes a link to references in this area.

http://www.pareonline.net

PARE (Practical Assessment, Research and Evaluation) is an online journal supported in part by the Department of Measurement, Statistics, and Evaluation at the University of Maryland, College Park. Aimed at education professionals, it provides access to refereed articles concerning evaluation, assessment, research, and teaching practice.

http://www.oerl.sri.com

The Online Evaluation Research Library is funded by the National Science Foundation and provides a catalogue of plans, instruments, and reports from past and current project evaluations as well as guidelines for improving evaluation.

http://www.socialresearchmethods.net

Bill Trochim's Web site provides an online textbook and handbook. This resource provides tutorials, simulations, and pointers for conducting research and evaluation.

Resource C

Taxonomy of Cognitive Objectives

A. Knowledge
   1. Specifics
   2. Ways and means of dealing with specifics
   3. Universals and abstractions

B. Comprehension
   1. Translation
   2. Interpretation
   3. Extrapolation

C. Application

D. Analysis
   1. Elements
   2. Relationships
   3. Organizational principles

E. Synthesis
   1. Unique communication
   2. Plan
   3. Derivations

F. Evaluation
   1. Using internal evidence
   2. Using external criteria

Resource D

Standards for Program Evaluations

These standards have been established by the Joint Committee on Standards for Educational Evaluation:

UTILITY STANDARDS

The utility standards are intended to ensure that an evaluation will serve the information needs of intended users.

U1 Stakeholder Identification

Persons involved in or affected by the evaluation should be identified, so that their needs can be addressed.

U2 Evaluator Credibility

The persons conducting the evaluation should be both trustworthy and competent to perform the evaluation, so that the evaluation findings achieve maximum credibility and acceptance.

U3 Information Scope and Selection

Information collected should be broadly selected to address pertinent questions about the program and be responsive to the needs and interests of clients and other specified stakeholders.

U4 Values Identification

The perspectives, procedures, and rationale used to interpret the findings should be carefully described, so that the bases for value judgments are clear.

U5 Report Clarity

Evaluation reports should clearly describe the program being evaluated, including its context, and the purposes, procedures, and findings of the evaluation, so that essential information is provided and easily understood.

U6 Report Timeliness and Dissemination

> Significant interim findings and evaluation reports should be disseminated to intended users, so that they can be used in a timely fashion.

U7 Evaluation Impact

> Evaluations should be planned, conducted, and reported in ways that encourage follow-through by stakeholders, so that the likelihood that the evaluation will be used is increased.

FEASIBILITY

The feasibility standards are intended to ensure that an evaluation will be realistic, prudent, diplomatic, and frugal.

F1 Practical Procedures

> The evaluation procedures should be practical, to keep disruption to a minimum while needed information is obtained.

F2 Political Viability

> The evaluation should be planned and conducted with anticipation of the different positions of various interest groups, so that their cooperation may be obtained and so that possible attempts by any of these groups to curtail evaluation operations or to bias or misapply the results can be averted or counteracted.

F3 Cost Effectiveness

> The evaluation should be efficient and produce information of sufficient value, so that the resources expended can be justified.

PROPRIETY

The propriety standards are intended to ensure that an evaluation will be conducted legally, ethically, and with due regard for the welfare of those involved in the evaluation as well as those affected by its results.

P1 Service Orientation

> Evaluations should be designed to assist organizations to address and effectively serve the needs of the full range of targeted participants.

P2 Formal Agreements

> Obligations of the formal parties to an evaluation (what is to be done, how, by whom, when) should be agreed to in writing, so that

these parties are obligated to adhere to all conditions of the agreement or formally to renegotiate it.

P3   Rights of Human Subjects

Evaluations should be designed and conducted to respect and protect the rights and welfare of human subjects.

P4   Human Interactions

Evaluators should respect human dignity and worth in their interactions with other persons associated with an evaluation, so that participants are not threatened or harmed.

P5   Complete and Fair Assessment

The evaluation should be complete and fair in its examination and recording of strengths and weaknesses of the program being evaluated, so that strengths can be built upon and problem areas addressed.

P6   Disclosure of Findings

The formal parties to an evaluation should ensure that the full set of evaluation findings along with pertinent limitations are made accessible to the persons affected by the evaluation and any others with expressed legal rights to receive the results.

P7   Conflict of Interest

Conflict of interest should be dealt with openly and honestly, so that it does not compromise the evaluation processes and results.

P8   Fiscal Responsibility

The evaluator's allocation and expenditure of resources should reflect sound accountability procedures and otherwise be prudent and ethically responsible, so that expenditures are accounted for and appropriate.

ACCURACY

The accuracy standards are intended to ensure that an evaluation will reveal and convey technically adequate information about the features that determine worth of merit of the program being evaluated.

A1   Program Documentation

The program being evaluated should be described and documented clearly and accurately so that the program is clearly identified.

A2   Context Analysis

The context in which the program exists should be examined in enough detail so that its likely influences on the program can be identified.

A3   Described Purposes and Procedures

The purposes and procedures of the evaluation should be monitored and described in enough detail so that they can be identified and assessed.

A4   Defensible Information Sources

The sources of information used in a program evaluation should be described in enough detail so that the adequacy of the information can be assessed.

A5   Valid Information

The information-gathering procedures should be chosen or developed and then implemented so that they will ensure that the interpretation arrived at is valid for the intended use.

A6   Reliable Information

The information-gathering procedures should be chosen or developed and then implemented so that they will ensure that the information obtained is sufficiently reliable for the intended use.

A7   Systematic Information

The information collected, processed, and reported in an evaluation should be systematically reviewed and any errors found should be corrected.

A8   Analysis of Quantitative Information

Quantitative information in an evaluation should be appropriately and systematically analyzed so that evaluation questions are effectively answered.

A9   Analysis of Qualitative Information

Qualitative information in an evaluation should be appropriately and systematically analyzed so that evaluation questions are effectively answered.

A10   Justified Conclusions

The conclusions reached in an evaluation should be explicitly justified, so that stakeholders can assess them.

A11   Impartial Reporting

Reporting procedures should guard against distortion caused by personal feelings and biases of any party to the evaluation so that evaluation reports fairly reflect the evaluation findings.

A12 Metaevaluation

> The evaluation itself should be formatively and summatively evaluated against these and other pertinent standards so that its conduct is appropriately guided and, on completion, stakeholders can closely examine its strengths and weaknesses.

Guidelines and illustrative cases to assist evaluation participants in meeting each of these standards are provided in *The Program Evaluation Standards* (Joint Committee on Standards for Educational Evaluation, 1994). The illustrative cases are based in a variety of educational settings, including schools, universities, medical and health care fields, the military, business and industry, the government, and law.

References

Awsumb-Nelson, C. (2001). *Strengthening your school's accountability plan: A technical assistance manual for Cleveland Community Schools*. The Evaluation Center, Western Michigan University. Available at http://www.wmich.edu/evalctr/charter/cleveland/accountability_manual.pdf

Airasian, P. W. (1997). *Classroom assessment*. New York: McGraw-Hill.

Banta, T. W. (2004). *Portfolio assessment: Uses, cases, scoring, and impact.* Indianapolis, IN: Jossey-Bass.

Bloom, B. S., Englehart, M. D., Furst, E. J., Hill, W. H., & Krathwohl, D. R. (1956). *Taxonomy of educational objectives: Handbook 1. Cognitive domain.* New York: David McKay.

Bracey, J. (2004). The 13th Bracey Report on the condition of public education. *Phi Delta Kappan*, 148–164. Retrieved April 15, 2005, from http://www.america-tomorrow.com/bracey/EDDRA/k0310bra.pdf

Chubb, J., & Moe, J. (1990). *Politics, markets, and America's schools*. Washington, DC: Brookings Institute.

Crew, R. E., & Anderson, M. R. (2003). Accountability and performance in charter schools in Florida: A theory-based evaluation. *American Journal of Evaluation, 24*(2), 189–212.

Davidson, E. J. (2001). The meta-learning organization: A model and methodology for evaluating organizational learning capacity. *Dissertation Abstracts International, 62* (5), 1882A. (UMI No. 3015945)

Dillman, D. A. (2000). *Mail and Internet surveys: The tailored design method* (2nd ed.). New York: John Wiley & Sons.

Fink, A. (2005). *How to conduct surveys: A step-by-step guide* (3rd ed.). Thousand Oaks, CA: Sage.

Fitzpatrick, J. L., Sanders, J. R., & Worthen, B. R. (2004). *Program evaluation* (3rd ed.). Boston: Allyn & Bacon.

Fowler, F. J., Jr., & Mangione, T. W. (1990). *Standardized survey interviewing: Minimizing interviewer-related error*. Newbury Park, CA: Sage.

Gall, M. D., Borg, W. R., & Gall, J. P. (1996). *Educational research* (6th ed.). New York: Longman.

Gonick, L., & Smith, W. (1993). *The cartoon guide to statistics*. New York: HarperPerennial

Herman, J. L. (Ed.). (1987). *Program evaluation kit* (2nd ed.). Newbury Park, CA: Sage.

Hopkins, K. D. (1998). *Educational and psychological measurement and evaluation* (8th ed.). Boston: Allyn & Bacon.

Hopkins, K. D., Hopkins, B. R., & Glass, G. V. (1996). *Basic statistics for the behavioral sciences* (3rd ed.). Boston: Allyn & Bacon.

Huberman, M., & Miles, M. B. (Eds.). (2002). *The qualitative researcher's companion.* Thousand Oaks, CA: Sage.

Jaeger, R. M. (1990). *Statistics: A spectator sport* (2nd ed.). Newbury Park, CA: Sage.

Joint Committee on Standards for Educational Evaluation. (1994). *The program evaluation standards* (2nd ed.). Thousand Oaks, CA: Sage.

Legislative Office of Education Oversight. (2003). *Community schools in Ohio: Final report on student performance, parent satisfaction, and accountability.* Columbus, OH: Author

Miron, G., & Horn, J. (2002). *Evaluation of Connecticut charter schools and the charter school initiative: Final report.* Kalamazoo: The Evaluation Center, Western Michigan University.

Newman, D. L., & Brown, R. D. (1996). *Applied ethics for program evaluation.* Thousand Oaks, CA: Sage.

Newmann, F. M., Smith, B., Allensworth, E., & Bryk, A. S. (2001). Instructional program coherence: What it is and why it should guide school improvement policy. *Educational Evaluation and Policy Analysis, 23*(4), 297–321.

Patton, M. Q. (1997). *Utilization-focused evaluation* (3rd ed.) Thousand Oaks, CA: Sage.

Patton, M. Q. (2001). *Qualitative research & evaluation methods* (3rd ed.). Thousand Oaks, CA: Sage.

Robinson, J. P., Shaver, P. R., & Wrightsman, L. S. (Eds.). (1991). *Measures of personality and social psychological attitudes.* New York: Academic Press.

Stufflebeam, D. L. (1969). Evaluation as enlightenment for decision making. In W. A. Beaty (Ed.), *Improving assessment and an inventory of measures of affective behavior.* Washington, DC: Association for Supervision and Curriculum Development.

Stufflebeam, D. L. (2001). *Evaluation models. New directions for evaluation, No. 89.* San Francisco: Jossey-Bass.

Sullins, C. D., & Miron, G. (2005). *Challenges of starting and operating charter schools: A multicase study.* Kalamazoo: The Evaluation Center, Western Michigan University. Retrieved from http://www.wmich.edu/evalctr/charter/cs_challenges_report.pdf.

Torres, R., Preskill, H. S., & Piontek, M. E. (2005). *Evaluation strategies for communicating and reporting: Enhancing learning in organizations* (2nd ed.). Thousand Oaks, CA: Sage.

United Way of America. (1996). *Measuring program outcomes.* Alexandria, VA: Author.

W. K. Kellogg Foundation. (2001). *W. K. Kellogg Foundation logic model development guide.* Available online at http://www.wkkf.org/Pubs/Tools/Evaluation/Pub3669.pdf

Webb, E. J., Campbell, D. T., Schwartz, R. D., & Sechrest, L. (2000). *Unobtrusive measures* (Rev. ed.). Thousand Oaks, CA: Sage.

Weber, R. P. (1990). *Basic content analysis (quantitative applications in the social sciences).* Thousand Oaks, CA: Sage.

Wheeler, P., Haertel, G. D., & Scriven, M. (1992). *Teacher evaluation glossary.* Kalamazoo: CREATE Project, The Evaluation Center, Western Michigan University. Retrieved from http://www.wmich.edu/evalctr/ess/glossary/

Index

**CORWIN
PRESS**

The Corwin Press logo—a raven striding across an open book—represents the union of courage and learning. Corwin Press is committed to improving education for all learners by publishing books and other professional development resources for those serving the field of PreK–12 education. By providing practical, hands-on materials, Corwin Press continues to carry out the promise of its motto: **"Helping Educators Do Their Work Better."**